Pet Power

Amazing true stories of animal bravery and devotion

Tess Cuming & David Wolstencroft

Ebury Press
London

'Pet Power' is a Prospect Pictures production for Meridian Broadcasting

First published in 1997

1 3 5 7 9 10 8 6 4 2

First published in the United Kingdom in 1997 by Ebury Press
Random House, 20 Vauxhall Bridge Road, London SW1V 2SA

Random House Australia (Pty) Limited
20 Alfred Street, Milsons Point, Sydney,
New South Wales 2061, Australia

Random House New Zealand Limited
18 Poland Road, Glenfield, Auckland 10, New Zealand

Random House South Africa (Pty) Limited
Endulini, 5a Jubilee Road, Parktown 2193, South Africa

Random House UK Limited Reg. No. 954009

A CIP catalogue record for this book is available from the British
Library.

ISBN 0 09 185328 1

Project editor Emma Callery
Designed by Jerry Goldie Graphic Design

Printed and bound in the UK by Butler and Tanner Ltd, Frome,
Somerset

Contents

Introduction

PET POWER IS ALL ABOUT THE GOOD THAT ANIMALS DO. MORE THAN ANY other country, Britain is a nation of animal lovers. At the last count, over 7 million of us own a dog, and about half a million more own a cat. That's before we include the million or so horses, parrots, budgies, hamsters, rabbits, gerbils, and other pets that share our lives.

Every day, across the country, countless numbers of pets are involved in acts of true bravery and devotion. Some do this work as part of their training,

others act out of sheer natural instinct to protect and care for their human friends. 'Pet Power' honours these unsung heroes and tells some of their astonishing stories for the first time.

It was apparent from the very first day of production that 'Pet Power' was going to be a very special kind of television show. The office was literally deluged with phone calls and letters from pet owners, and nearly every person had an exceptional story to tell. From

the length and breadth of the British Isles, the 'Pet Power' team learned of astonishing feats of bravery, and fine acts of kindness, strength, perseverance, willpower and loyalty. It was enough of a task to wade through the sheer volume of material, let alone decide which ones to include in the filming. But, finally, the team narrowed it down to a number of stories that were simply too extraordinary to pass over.

These are the stories you are about to read. Stories where pets have gone far beyond the call of duty to help others. Stories where lives have been saved, disasters averted. Stories where an animal has brought love and affection to those in real need.

One of the most amazing things about 'Pet Power' is that it is the first programme of its kind. Throughout history, the unconditional love that pets have given their human friends has been documented, but rarely has it been seen as a cause for true celebration. 'Pet Power' is the first major series to rectify that by highlighting the ceaseless and unselfish contributions animals have made and continue to make to our lives.

This book is dedicated to those pets, and to all the other animal heroes out there, who remain uncelebrated and unrecognised.

Tess Cuming and David Wolstencroft

TV Reconstruction

A Lassie with a Lamp

THIS IS THE STORY OF SOPHIE, A VERY SPECIAL GOLDEN LABRADOR WITH A unique talent. Her owner, Ashford Price, manages the Dan-yr-Ogof caves near Swansea, a major Welsh tourist site. In winter, however, the caves are closed for repair work.

When Sophie was a puppy, it was natural for her to follow her master around wherever he went. Ashford would often find himself helping out with any electrical and concrete work that needed doing, and like as not there would be young Sophie by his side. Bit by bit she would venture further and further into the cave system, until eventually she came to spend the whole day underground.

One day, a school party came to visit the caves from Bristol, and Sophie was sent in with them to add to the trip. She was a huge success, a happy companion for the young visitors. She seemed completely comfortable with the exercise, and it got Ashford thinking. Perhaps he should see just how far this dog's natural affinity could be taken. Perhaps, with time, Sophie's evident enjoyment of the caves could be developed to perform a useful function. At the end of the working day, Ashford would have to make certain that no one was left in the labyrinthine passages within the cave system. With Sophie, perhaps that laborious task could be made a little easier.

That Sophie even put one paw inside the caves is remarkable in itself. Caves are a naturally hostile environment for dogs. The temperature, the

Sophie's skills as a cave rescue dog are unique.

quality of the air, and the smell all conspire against an animal's natural instincts. Almost every other dog that dared to venture into the relative darkness would about-turn within a few steps. Sophie's twin sister, Misty, would hardly come near the entrance if given half a chance. Sophie, however, came to love the caves, and could be found underground on hot summer days of her own volition, in an attempt to stay cool.

Her training was slow and steady. Trails were laid down for her (chocolate was a great incentive) as Ashford determined just how far into the cave's huge system of passages she would go. They treated it like a game, and often Ashford felt Sophie was encouraging him to go that little bit further. She was certainly a willing pupil.

Eventually, she was taken on a complete tour of the cave system. She passed through little holes, small lakes, and behind waterfalls experiencing cold, wet, and complete darkness. Whatever test Ashford set, Sophie passed with flying colours. Then, one day in April 1995, a harmless game between dog and owner found a far more serious use.

Pet File

Name: Sophie.

Age: 6 years.

Likes: Swimming in mountain rivers; her Ninja Turtle soft toy; chocolate.

Dislikes: Being towelled down after swimming.

Hobbies: Chasing squirrels; sneaking onto Ashford's bed for a sleep.

Simon Evans had worked at the caves for a number of years. It was customary for him to go into the caves in the evening for a shift of up to eight hours. The main showcase cave needs to be cable free, so all light cables get taken through the myriad of passages that feed off it. The cables are dragged through holes which are often no more than 30 cm wide. But Simon is not called 'the ferret' for nothing. A sleek man of 27, his whippet-like build makes him the ideal shape for wriggling through tight spots. But he was soon to find himself in a spot where no amount of wriggling would help him.

His duty this particular night was some rewiring, a straightforward job that he had done many times before. He started work with a colleague, but

RECONSTRUCTION ■ ■ ■ ■ ■ ■ ■ ■ ■ ■ ■ ■ ■ ■ ■ ■

Sophie knew the cave system well.

eventually they each went their separate ways. Wearing his hard hat with battery light, he started work, and had been hard at it for over four hours when he opted for a passage that initially looked safe as houses. As he crawled through, he noticed sand and silt deposits on the roof and walls caused by a recent flood.

It was then that the walls came tumbling down.

His wriggling had loosened the already precarious deposits above and around him. In a second, they had plummeted to the ground, trapping Simon's body around his trunk. The problem now was not so much the weight, as the volume: Simon was completely wedged in. But he didn't panic. He couldn't believe that he was trapped, yet this soon became apparent. Staying calm, he knew that the more he struggled, the worse things could get.

'I know from experience that if you do get stuck in something, the more you twist about the more you get stuck fast,' he explains. 'The easiest thing to do is just to try and relax.'

Simon could still move his arms and legs, but he was also sweating profusely. 'It wasn't very pleasant at all,' he recalls. ' And the only thing I could do was wait.'

As time wore on, Simon focused on the belief that someone would find him, and he continued to kick his feet to keep his circulation going and to keep warm. But, inevitably, his thoughts turned to his family, and these were his darker moments. 'I just tried to push them to the back of my mind,' he remembers.

Back in the office, 10 o'clock came and went, and Ashford realised that something was wrong. 'With the caves you can spend a lot of time fiddling about, so I waited another half an hour before picking up the phone.'

Then, together with two other employees, Ashford began walking into the caves. As a matter of routine, Sophie was by his side. Ashford wasn't sure if it would help, but he gave Sophie Simon's jacket to sniff. It was possible she might pick up the scent that way and so lead them to him.

Shouting Simon's name, the three men made slow progress around the myriad passageways of the caves. 'What we did first of all was go round the showcase quickly to make sure he wasn't just somewhere having his sandwiches,' recalls Ashford, 'and that's when I did get concerned.'

The only way the men could proceed was to stop at each passageway and search. Many of these were too small to investigate. 'We were literally having to check each section he could be in,' explains Ashford, 'I couldn't pin down where he'd gone.' An hour into the search, and they were no closer to locating him. Simon could have been anywhere. And that was when Sophie disappeared. 'She scampered off,' remembers Ashford, 'and she didn't come back.'

It was only a matter of minutes before the men heard her barking. Back in the tunnel, Simon was tapping his feet to stimulate the circulation. He had been trapped for five

RECONSTRUCTION ■ ■ ■ ■ ■ ■

**Top: Sophie set off to find the missing man.
Above: Simon was more than grateful to his canine rescuer.**

On the scent

- Did you know that most dogs are more than fifty times better at smelling things than us: the average canine has around 220 million scent receptors in its nose and 7 m squared of nasal membrane. We only have around 5 million, and half a metre!
- Most dogs have such highly-developed scenting abilities that they can recognise smells so dilute, even the most advanced of scientific instruments cannot measure them.
- In October 1988, a German Shepherd owned by Essex police sniffed out 2 tonnes of cannabis worth £6 million when it was sent to a remote cottage on the outskirts of Harlow.

THE INCREDIBLE JOURNEY In 1925, Sauer, a Doberman trained by Detective-Sergeant Herbert Kruger, tracked a stock thief 100 miles across the Great Karroo, South Africa, by scent alone.

hours. But now he felt something at his toes. It was Sophie, wagging her tail.

Following the sound of Sophie's barks, Ashford and the other men had little trouble in locating Simon. With a couple of tugs, he was free and although the men were elated, it was Sophie who made the biggest fuss of Simon, leaping around excitedly. Simon knew all about Sophie, she was a loved and popular dog who was petted by all the staff. 'But the thought never entered my mind that she would find me,' he explains.

Simon was numb and cold, but otherwise in one piece. He hugged the dog and made a huge fuss of her. 'Everyone went bananas, but I went double bananas,' continues Simon. 'There are passages all over and they didn't have the manpower to send someone down each one to look for me. Luckily though, they had Sophie.'

Sophie is a unique dog, and possibly the first and last cave rescue dog in Britain. Cave rescue teams don't use dogs as part of their team because they recognise the fact that dogs do not take to the environment in which they work. In Sophie's case it was a unique set of circumstances, which combined to make the rescue a success.

Simon has no doubt that the outcome would not have been quite as happy if it hadn't been for Sophie, and he and she remain the greatest friends to this day. 'I don't think she really realised what she'd done,' he says. 'But I certainly did. Sophie is just the softest, most loveable dog. She's a great fan of chocolate, and afterwards I made sure she had plenty!'

TV Reconstruction

Guinness and the Chocolate Bar

JESS YATES HAD ALWAYS WANTED A DOG. HE HAD ALSO ALWAYS WANTED TO BE in the Navy. But working as an aircrewman in a Navy flying squad meant he was always away from home, on missions around the world, and having a dog just wasn't an option.

After flying for ten years, Fate took a hand in Jess's career, and he was diagnosed as diabetic. 'I was told I couldn't fly any more,' says Jess, 'and needless to say, I was absolutely gutted.' The Navy offered him a desk job instead, but, as Jess observes, 'I didn't want to fly a desk. So I took a security job on an airbase before my medical discharge.'

But there was a silver lining to his disappointment. At last, he could own a dog. After reading an advertisement in a free weekly newspaper in his home town of Sherborne, Dorset, Jess went to visit a puppy litter of six or seven Collie/Labrador cross breeds. 'There was one there, a black one, he was the runt,' explains Jess. 'He had half the fur missing from his head, and no one really wanted him. But I said I'd take him.'

Jess called his dog Guinness, and the two of them became inseparable. They were frequent visitors to the cottage of Pete Prescott and his dog Gypsy.

Pet File

Pet name:
Guinness.
Age: 7 years.
Likes: Yellow
cricket ball; his
own bunk bed,
which he
sleeps in;
chocolate bars;
a well-known
brand of stout.
Dislikes:
Bathtime.
Hobbies:
Leaning on
people; table-
hopping in the
pub; fetching
anything.

**Guinness is good-
looking – and he
knows it!**

Pete was a friend of Jess's from 846 Squadron in Yeovilton, the two men had often flown missions together. True to form, their two dogs quickly became good friends. 'Guinness used to stay with us when Jess went on holiday,' recalls Pete. In fact, Gypsy taught him to swim when he was a puppy.'

In early April 1990, Pete was on Easter leave and asked his friend for help. He was renovating his cottage and building a large dry stone wall in his back garden. Jess happily agreed, and early one overcast Spring morning, the two men got to work.

'It wasn't boiling hot weather,' remembers Pete, 'but because we were moving these slabs and mixing the mortar, we were bringing up quite a sweat.' The two friends worked all day, watched, as ever, by their faithful canines.

As a diabetic, Jess has to be very careful about how much energy he expends. 'Basically, you need to be sure you're putting in as much as you're taking out.' says Jess. Although he had been working hard, Jess was sure he had monitored his blood sugar and felt fine. The job was done, and the two men calculated they had shifted over four tons of stone between them.

When he arrived home that night, Jess felt very tired. After pottering around the house for a short while, he decided to go to bed. The time was 11pm. 'Usually I'm very good about checking I've got enough supplies,' Jess explains, 'things like chocolate and sugary drinks in case I wake up during the night and need a dose of sugar.' He kept them on a shelf behind the bed, easily within arm's reach. Just in case.

Jess and Pete were in the same Naval squadron in Yeovilton.

But because he was tired, Jess only glanced at his bedside supplies. Seeing the familiar wrappers, he was satisfied. He could go to sleep. And after such a hard day, sleep came very easily.

But Jess was not alone in his bedroom. The ever-doting Guinness was only too happy to sleep on the floor beside the bed. Sometimes, during the night, he would creep up on to the mattress, and Jess would often wake to find him there. Luckily for Jess, on this night, that is exactly where he was.

At two-thirty that morning, Jess snapped awake. The first thing he was aware of was water – and lots of it. 'I thought the water bed had burst,' recalls Jess, 'there was just so much liquid.' But it wasn't water. It was sweat.

Jess was suffering from extremely low blood sugar. Known as 'hypoglycaemia', this is a common but potentially dangerous condition. It was one that Jess was used to: 'I usually get early warning signs, being irritable, breaking out in a sweat. But being so tired, I guess I had bypassed that stage.'

In fact, Jess soon realised he was in more than a spot of trouble. He reached over for the bottle of energy drink by his bed. But it was empty. He had mistaken the coloured base of the bottle for the liquid itself. 'I thought, "never mind",' remembers Jess, '"let's try the chocolate."' Jess moved his hand over to the wrappers. But they too were empty.

The implications were very serious. Unless he could get some sugar – and fast – his own lack of sugar would cause him to move into a coma. And after going into a coma, there was no telling what might happen.

Now there was only one thing for it. Jess would have to go downstairs to the kitchen, where a large stash of chocolate was piled on the counter. But when he tried to get out of bed, he discovered to his horror that he couldn't move his legs. The lack of sugar was preventing his brain sending the right signals to his muscles.

'I tried not to panic,' remembers Jess, 'because the more you panic, the more energy you waste. I guess I just thought of a plan of action because I had to.' Jess grabbed a chocolate wrapper, and called Guinness to his side. Guinness was already concerned at his master's condition, and obeyed immediately. Jess pushed the wrapper towards his nose. 'Go on, Guinness, fetch!' he said, hoping the dog would understand.

To Jess's delight Guinness turned on a sixpence and hared off downstairs. Moments later, he returned, triumphant, wagging his tail. Jess craned his neck to catch a glimpse of the familiar wrapper that would spell the end of his troubles. But Guinness had returned empty-mouthed. 'That's when I got even more anxious,' explains Jess. 'Guinness thought it was all a bit of game.'

Realising time was running out, Jess had no option but to try again. He fumbled among the wrappers once more. Finding a specimen with a small streak of chocolate still present, he called Guinness once more, and rubbed the wrapper on his nose.

'Guinness sometimes gets given a chocolate bar as a treat,' says Jess, 'but he also knows that he's not allowed to take anything without permission.' Wagging his tail, Guinness left the room once more, and Jess was left alone, hoping his dog would understand that this wasn't a game any more.

Jess craned his neck to catch a glimpse of the familiar wrapper.

In a matter of seconds, Guinness was back on the bed again, and this time, he dropped a familiar black wrapper on the pillow next to Jess. A Mars Bar. Jess grabbed at the wrapping, and wolfed down the chocolate. 'It was just enough to get my legs working again,' he remembers. 'I managed to get myself downstairs, and sort myself out properly with some energy drink.'

Alone in the kitchen, dazed, and soaked through with sweat, Jess sat in

RECONSTRUCTION ■ ■ ■ ■ ■ ■ ■ ■ ■ ■ ■ ■ ■ ■ ■

Top left: Guinness grabbed the chocolate bar from the table.

Top right: He wasted no time taking it to Jess.

Right: Jess knows Guinness is a very special dog.

the darkness. He was alive. And the reason he was alive was now pushing his nose under his master's arm – Guinness. 'I picked him up and gave him a big hug,' says Jess, 'I probably cried a little too.'

The next morning, Pete Prescott was one of the first to hear of Jess's ordeal. 'At first I said, oh come on, Jess,' he recalls, 'but I could tell over the phone how emotional he was, and I thought, "hang on, this bloke's serious." So I jumped in the car and went straight over.'

Unaware of his growing fame, Guinness is now happily sharing Jess's house with Nicky, Jess's girlfriend, and her dogs Ursula and Angus. He enjoys visiting the Cross Keys in Sherborne for a bowl of his namesake tipple, and making as many friends as he possibly can amongst the regulars. 'People now say hello to him before they say hello to me,' laughs Jess.

But with a friend like Guinness, Jess certainly isn't complaining.

Pet Casebook

• •

A Helping Paw

SALLY THE GOLDEN RETRIEVER MUST QUALIFY AS ONE OF THE WORLD'S MOST waggy dogs. Now, most of the dogs in Britain wag their tails when they are happy, but there are those who feel that this is far too limiting, and can't help but wag their entire bodies! Sally is one of those dogs. Almost every minute of the day, her entire hind quarters sashay from side to side in celebration, a joyful canine hula that simply says: 'I love my life'. It's this kind of ready commitment and selfless attitude that makes an enormous difference in the lives of thousands of people. Like Neil and Ann Jackson, who have had Sally since she was a little puppy.

Neil suffers from multiple sclerosis, a debilitating disease that can strike anyone, at any time. Eighteen years ago, Neil was taking a dog, a cat and a rabbit for a walk when he began to behave as if he was drunk. He wondered what it was, and sent for the doctor. It wasn't until two years later that he was diagnosed as having MS.

As Neil's condition worsened, Ann found herself having to help her husband more and more. There were hard times, but Sally and Emma, their two Retrievers, helped raise their spirits when they could. Although belonging to the same breed, the dogs' natures were radically different. While Emma was content to lie around the house all day, Sally showed a keen intelligence and interest in the world around her, often alerting Ann to the ringing of the cooker timer if she was out in the garden.

Sally the milkmaid helps her owner Neil.

As a young dog, Sally was, as Neil puts it, 'no trouble whatsoever'. Quiet, and obedient, she was very affectionate, very quickly. 'Sally wanted to be part of the family,' explains Ann, 'she was a natural helper.'

The thought of utilising Sally's natural talents didn't take root in Ann's mind until a particular incident occurred. 'Neil had quite a bad fall one day,' she explains, 'he was in the drive for about half an hour. Nobody knew he was there. Because Sally was so bright and able to think for herself, I had the idea that we could teach her to fetch me if he fell again.'

The thought stayed with Ann until one day she happened to mention it to her friend Katy Patmore, a dog trainer. Katy then told her about a woman called Val Strong, who was thinking about setting up a scheme for the disabled, where existing pet dogs would be trained to aid their owners. It would be called Support Dogs. It sounded like the perfect opportunity for a dog like Sally.

'The thing we wanted to do was just train her to fetch the phone,' recalls Neil. 'At that particular time I could walk with sticks, but I was very, very slow, so when the telephone rang, I had to get out of my chair and walk to the phone, and by the time I got there it had stopped ringing.' Neither Neil nor Ann had any idea that by the end of Sally's training, simply answering the telephone would be hardly scratching the surface of her abilities.

Right from the start, Val Strong warned both Neil and Ann that the course would be tough going: it would last 12 months, and during that time they would be working just as hard as the dog. Each Wednesday afternoon, both owner and dog would work together on a particular skill area. Then, during the week, they would practise, and practise again, ready for the next meeting. Only when the dog and owner had mastered that particular skill could they move on. In fact, Val was training both Neil and Sally to work together as a team.

'When Sally first started her training,' remembers Ann, 'although she regarded it as a game all the time, she used to get very tired and she used to stop and sort of look at you as if to say, 'I don't want to do any more.' But after four or five weeks, Sally began to recognise the training days, and she would happily walk towards the car with her tail wagging.'

Pet File

Pet name: Sally.
Age: 6 years.
Likes: Working; sharing a banana with Ann and Neil; chocolate; munching chestnuts in the nearby woods; having bath's.
Dislikes: Boxing on television.
Hobbies: Opening doors for fellow pet Emma when she barks to be let through.

As her training progressed from strength to strength, it was clear to everyone concerned that Sally simply adored her new job. 'She absolutely wants to work all the time,' continues Ann, 'In fact, sometimes if Neil isn't there, it's quite hard trying to think of things she can help with. She'll sort of look at you and say, "is there anything you want doing?"'

There was, however, a more problematic element to the training process. Although Sally was working with Neil, she was actually Ann's dog. Emma,

RECONSTRUCTION ◼ ◼ ◼ ◼ ◼ ◼ ◼ ◼ ◼ ◼ ◼ ◼ ◼ ◼

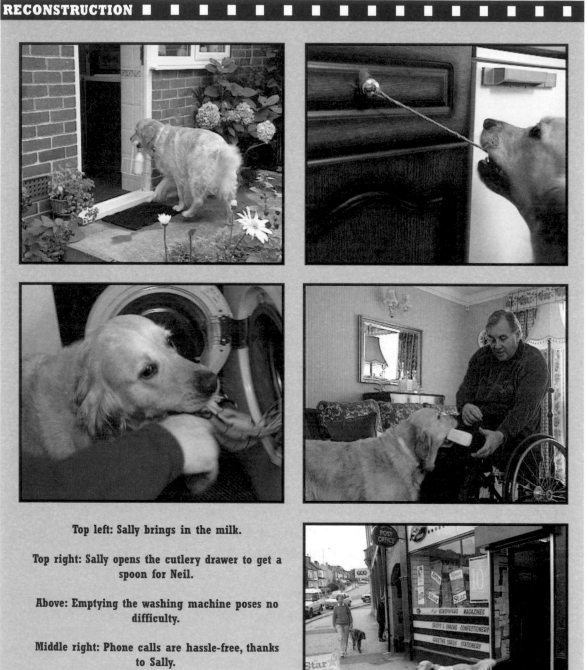

Top left: Sally brings in the milk.

Top right: Sally opens the cutlery drawer to get a spoon for Neil.

Above: Emptying the washing machine poses no difficulty.

Middle right: Phone calls are hassle-free, thanks to Sally.

Bottom right: Sally goes on one of her regular errands to the post office.

Sally showed a keen intelligence from an early stage and proved a natural helper.

their other Retriever, was officially Neil's. If Sally was to work properly with Neil, it was going to be important to transfer her loyalty to him. In effect, they had to swap allegiances, a very painful process, especially for Ann: 'I had to ignore Sally, and Sally would sit at the side of me and she would look with sorrowful eyes. "What have I done? Have I done something wrong?", and I would have to turn away.' In order to complete the transfer process, all of the food, affection and walks now had to come from Neil. Happily, Neil, Ann and Sally came through this difficult time with flying colours. Sally eventually tranferred her affections to Neil, and a special bond now exists between all three of them.

Soon the day came that the L-plates came off, and Sally was allowed to wear the distinctive yellow coat of a fully-qualified Support Dog. It's a job she now takes very seriously indeed. 'When she gets her coat on, there seems to be a change in her,' says Neil. 'She seems to be calmer and it's as though she's thinking, "Right, I've got my coat on, I'm working."' Neil says that Sally is also very sensitive to the moods of her new partner. 'If she senses I'm having an off day, she'll go and lie in a corner until I want something,' continues Neil. 'I try and give her rest times more than any other thing, but Sally's the type of dog who just loves working.'

In fact, her workaholic nature often needs to be kept in check. For Sally, playtime means the uniform comes off, and Neil and Ann often enjoy taking her down to the nearby park to play with a ball. After all, as Neil observes, 'she is first and foremost a pet.'

The working day of a Support Dog is long and full of activity. The day begins for Sally as soon as Neil wakes up. She sleeps at the bottom of the bed, and as soon as Neil is awake she will come and say good morning. Sally then makes her way into the kitchen, where she finds Ann. Sally will then deliver Neil his breakfast in bed, allowing Ann to get on with her work. 'I will put Neil's cereal and so on in to a plastic dish, which she takes in to Neil,' explains Ann. 'She also takes his cutlery, and she waits until he's finished breakfast.'

After breakfast, Sally will fetch Neil his paper once he is up and dressed, followed by a short walk in the park. On Monday mornings, Sally accompanies Neil down to the Post Office, where access is difficult for Neil's wheelchair. She is happy to wait her turn in the queue, and collects Neil's pension in a special satchel.

VALIANT VETERAN
Labrador Retriever Cindi-Cleo notched up the longest ever period of active service for a guide dog when she finished her stint of 14 years, 8 months in 1987 helping owner Aron Barr of Tel Aviv, Israel.

For the rest of the day, Sally is able to respond to any need which Neil might have at any particular time. She can fetch the telephone, switch lights on and off, open drawers ... and all done with a joyful wag of the tail that defies gravity.

In her support of Neil, Sally also frees Ann to have more control over her life, too. 'Since Sally qualified, it has given both of us much more independence,' Ann explains. 'Neil's got more confidence now he's got Sally. He often doesn't like to ask for things, now he can get Sally to help.'

All in all, Sally has made a lasting impression on their lives, supporting both husband and wife in equal measure. 'She's most definitely a family support dog,' says Ann. 'I really can't imagine life without her.' Neil agrees: 'I'm sure that many people would just stand in awe, with their mouths wide open, at some of the things she can do.'

TV Reconstruction

Sparky and the Cows

ANTI-SOCIAL, WILFUL, DISOBEDIENT ... IT WAS HARDLY THE PERFECT character reference for a domestic pet. But sometimes the most unlikely of personalities can prove a hero, as the Douglas family of Welwyn Garden City were to discover.

Corinne and Geoff Douglas knew from day one they had taken on a strong-willed dog when they collected Sparky, an Ibizan hound from their local Blue Cross Rescue Centre. But they little anticipated the problems that would soon follow his arrival.

From the very start, Sparky refused to obey the most basic of commands. It was quite obvious he had never been out on a lead before. Their vet recommended dog training classes, but they seemed to have little effect. Despite his obvious intelligence, Sparky seemed a reluctant pupil. 'He was as good as gold for the first half an hour,' explains Corinne. 'But after that he was thoroughly bored. It was an absolute nightmare.'

Back home it was the same story: daily walks regularly ended in a tussle, and mealtimes turned into a battle of wills as the family tried to coax the hesitant dog into eating. There was no doubt that Sparky was more than a handful.

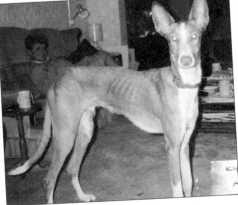

A rare moment of obedience for an under-nourished young Sparky, shortly after his arrival in the Douglas household.

Pet File

Pet name: Sparky.

Age: 4 ½ years.

Likes: Mature cheddar cheese; his black Labrador girlfriend, Poppy; Corinne's grandchildren.

Dislikes: Any titbits that aren't cheese.

Hobbies: Playing football; his favourite hidey hole in the garden; sitting on the sofa next to Corinne watching TV.

The Ibizan hound

Origins: The origins of this hound are believed to be the island of Ibiza, off the eastern coast of Spain.

Appearance: Similar to a Greyhound with its tall, lean body, and long head and tail.

Height/weight: average 65 cm/about 23 kg.

Characteristics:

- Not aggressive and very sensitive to scolding, making it the perfect housedog when there are kids around.
- Needs lots of space.
- Feels the cold.
- Hunts by scent rather than sight.

Worst of all was his anti-social behaviour. Shunning the love and affection lavished on him by the three Douglas children, the dog shied away from being stroked and made little attempt to seek the family's company, preferring solitude. Far from becoming a loving part of the household, as Corinne and Geoff had hoped, Sparky seemed determined to remain an unhappy and very unwilling lodger.

'We cried buckets over him because he was so dreadful,' admits Corinne. 'We just didn't know what to do because he was such a nightmare.' The burden of keeping and caring for a dog like Sparky affected every member of the Douglas family. 'My daughters would say, "what are you doing with that dog? Why don't you take him back?"'

'We cried buckets over him because he was so dreadful.'

For nearly three years, the Douglas family battled on with their dysfunctional dog. Although Sparky was evidently highly intelligent, his will was against that of his owners. Corrine freely admits there were times when they nearly took him back. Even after the constant intervention of animal behaviourists and vets alike, the dog still refused to cooperate. It seemed as if nothing would calm down this canine.

In May 1996, Corinne decided to take a holiday. Her husband Geoff was away, and as she had a friend in Powys, Wales, she decided to venture off to visit her and take Sparky with her. 'We'd taken Sparky to Wales before,' she recalls, 'but this was the first time I had gone there with him on my own.'

She set off on the Tuesday morning, arriving in her friend Chris's village at half past two that afternoon. As Chris ran the village post office, Corinne arranged to come back at half past five, when she would have finished work. To pass the time, Corinne decided to take Sparky for a walk.

'We hadn't done a great deal of walking there,' recalls Corinne, 'but Chris told me that there were lots of footpaths around.' Armed with a map and an adventurous spirit, Corinne walked through the village and set off down the first footpath she came to.

Keeping Sparky tightly on the lead, she walked across two fields, enjoying the country air. As she approached the next field, Corinne noticed that it was home to a number of cows. She decided to press on. After all, her dog was on the lead, and it was a public footpath. It was perfectly safe. Corinne climbed over the stile, and continued her walk.

The field was large, and as she made progress along the path, Corinne could see there were a lot of cows on the far side, some with calves. 'I was walking along, and Sparky was walking beside me,' remembers Corinne. 'He was more interested in what rabbits were in the hedge.'

It was then that one particular cow began walking towards her. The cow was, in fact, a young black bullock. As it became more interested in Corinne, she kept her pace and remained quiet. But the bullock was undeterred and began gaining speed. 'I was just thinking, "go away, stupid thing," and went on walking', says Corinne. But the bullock kept coming. Corinne began to run.

The other cows in the field were now following the bullock's lead, and

RECONSTRUCTION

Right: The cows began to advance.

Bottom left: Corinne and Sparky were trapped.

Bottom right: It was an emotional reunion for Sparky and his mistress.

thundered towards a terrified Corinne. As they crowded around her, she realised there was no escape route back to the stile. It was then that Sparky decided to act. Although he was on the lead, he stood in front of his mistress, attempting to get in between her and the threatening herd. But his gesture – his first protective gesture towards his mistress – was in vain.

One of the larger cows hit Corinne square in the ribs. The force was considerable, and knocked her over. Suddenly to her other side, another cow was moving to strike her in the head. Putting up her arms to protect herself, Corinne felt the lead slip away.

'I thought, "this is it"', she recalls, '"I'll never see him again." He's never allowed off the lead.' But Corinne was also relieved. At least Sparky would be safe. He was so thin and wiry that a blow from a cow could fracture his ribs, or even break his leg. She watched as her dog ran between the legs of the cows, towards the middle of the field.

And then, something remarkable happened. Instead of continuing off into the countryside, Sparky stopped. And turned. And began to bark. 'I could see him through their legs,' remembers Corinne, 'I could see him watching me.' Sparky's barks had caught the attention of the cows, who were starting to back up the field towards

> **Sparky stopped. And turned. And began to bark.**

him. He was leading them away from Corinne. 'He'd run a bit, and then he'd turn round and look,' continued Corinne. 'So I got up and went towards the stile.' Corinne had found an escape route and with Sparky's help, she took her window of opportunity.

Staggering towards safety, Corinne's thoughts were still with her dog. But as she debated whether to call for him, Sparky took the initiative. 'I was four or five yards from the stile,' she recalls, 'and he came without me calling him. Then suddenly I saw the cows were coming with him.'

For the dog who never came when he was called, it was a turn-up for the books. But it was also the last thing Corinne wanted to happen. She had sustained an injury to her ribs. Unable to run, she could only look on in horror as the herd closed in around her once again. After all Sparky's efforts, it seemed that his well-meant rescue attempt was back-firing.

But as the mass of animals bore down on Corinne, Sparky conjured up another remarkable act of intelligence. 'As they got near me it was as if Sparky realised what he was doing,' Corinne explains, 'so he circled round and went back into the middle of the field again and began barking once more.'

What Sparky Did

Kevin MacNicholas is a Pet Behaviour Counsellor. Corinne once brought Sparky to see him at the height of the dog's difficulties:

'Sparky was presenting dominant types of behaviour – he was aloof, difficult and doing everything on his own terms. It's not an unusual pattern of behaviour in dogs I see. At the moment of the cow attack, though, something happened. When Corinne fell over, the usual channel of communication between dog and owner was lost. Sparky had to make a decision to keep the other animals – the cows – away from Corinne, his main resource. He acted quickly and with considerable intelligence.

'The radical change of behaviour in Sparky afterwards could be due to losing that resource – Corinne - for the first time. That loss changed the balance of power in their relationship.

'Later, when Sparky rejoined Corinne outside the field he learnt a new experience: bonding with his owner, and he also understood that it can be fun to interact. In that one moment the dog learnt a lot – how to control the cows, the loss of its communication system, and the reward of getting it back. And Corinne learnt too. She's indebted to the dog and her body language signals would have changed as a result. Once she saw Sparky behaving in a different way she, in turn, responded differently. The attack was a deciding moment for both of them.'

Sparky receives a medal and certificate of appreciation from the Blue Cross for his brave actions.

Sparky's renewed actions paid dividends. The cows turned again and duly followed their canine leader, who led them away from Corinne, making sure that this time she had made it all the way to the stile. 'As I went over the stile,' recalls Corinne, 'I realised he'd jumped over it and was next to me.'

Sitting down on the step, Corinne noticed for the first time that her face was bleeding. In fact, she was badly injured. But instead of leaving her and seeking further distractions, Sparky ventured over to Corinne, and began to lick her wounds. 'He'd licked my hands before, but he'd never shown any great affection,' Corrine explains. 'It was almost as if he sensed my hurt.'

Although dazed, Corinne picked up the lead and made her painful way back to her friend Chris. But the dog that had previously tugged on the leash now stopped his pulling altogether, walking patiently by her side. For some reason, Sparky's attitude to Corinne had changed. Perhaps it was a realisation that here was a woman who had put her faith in him. Or perhaps it was simply an incident that channelled his natural instincts into a good deed.

Whatever the real reasons, Sparky is now a more relaxed and attentive member of the Douglas family, a dog who is, without doubt, another inspiring example of Pet Power.

Dog Body Language

We are used to trying to read human body language, but do you know your way around these classic canine postures?

Ears and tail relaxed = calm, at ease

Ears up, tail up = alert, ready for action

Ears flattened, tail between legs = fright

Crouched with tail between legs = fear

Lying on back with raised leg
= submissive posture

Bowing, begging, licking hands/face
= happiness, playfulness

Hackles up, tail up, lips pulled back
= aggressive stance

Snarl exposing teeth, straight posture =
increased aggression

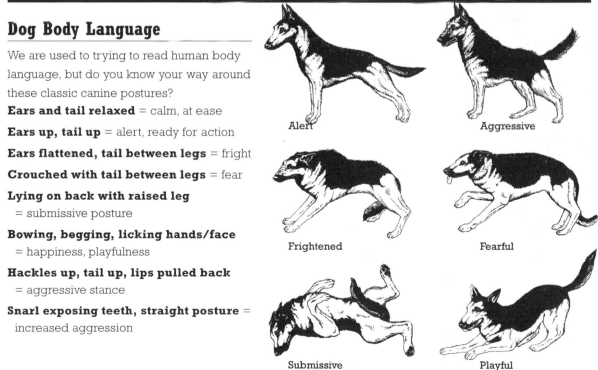

Alert

Aggressive

Frightened

Fearful

Submissive

Playful

TV Reconstruction

China the Wonder Horse

SMALL DECISIONS CAN HAVE BIG CONSEQUENCES. A WRONG TURNING HERE, a missed phone-call there – a split-second change of heart can sometimes turn everything upside down. For Mrs Sargent, a decision taken by a virtual stranger six years ago would later mean the difference between life and death.

For show-jumping enthusiast Mr Errol Flynn, it was just another of life's dilemmas: his beloved 16-year-old horse China had developed arthritis in his front feet. A vet pointed out that sometimes the condition resulted in a rapid deterioration if the horse wasn't exercised properly. He suggested that perhaps it would be best to put China to sleep. But Errol couldn't endure the thought of saying goodbye to his faithful horse before his time was up. Playful and lively, China seemed a long way from wanting to give up on life and his owner decided to go against the vet's suggestion.

The decision turned out to be the right one. Despite being given only two years to live at the most, China happily settled into life at the stables of farmer Martin Knowles near Colchester, Essex. With regular visits from his devoted owner Errol and a large acre-sized paddock to gallop across, Potter's Meadow was the perfect place for a graceful retirement. China flourished.

Across the fields in a nearby farm, 64 year-old Mrs Sargent was blissfully unaware of Errol and China's worries. A recent widow, she now had her one-and-half year old dog, Zoe (a Lhasa Apso), for company. Just after 9am on Wednesday, 21 February 1996, Mrs Sargent took Zoe for her morning walk. Her

Errol is devoted to his 16-year-old horse China.

usual route was to exercise her dog on the land at the back of the house, the Gosbeck's Archaelogical Park, an important site since the discovery of Roman remains there. To gain access to the park, she would use a gap in the fence at the back of her garden, and climb over a stile. This would allow her to walk along the bridle path that skirts the site.

That Wednesday morning was cold, windy and bright, a winter scene straight out of the picture books. It had been snowing heavily, some 60 cm deep in places, and Mrs Sargent was extremely wary of slipping. Some way along the path, she decided she would be more certain of her footing if she walked tight to the hedgerow that was running to her left. The snow was less deep there, and posed less of a risk.

Moments after leaving the path, Mrs Sargent's foot disappeared beneath the snow. 'The next thing I knew, I was tumbling forwards,' she explains, 'and I put out my hands to break my fall.'

In fact, Mrs Sargent had inadvertently stumbled into a fox hole, her right foot disappearing up to her knee. Stuck in the snow, on her hands and knees, she slowly eased her leg free. But in moving her limb, she realised there was now something new to contend with. Pain. 'I've never experienced anything like it before,' recalls Mrs Sargent, 'I knew I wouldn't be able to walk on it.'

Mrs Sargent didn't know it at the time, but she had broken her leg in a particularly nasty way. A piece of bone had splintered off from her tibia just

The paddock is large but the distance didn't stop China hearing Mrs Sargent's cries for help.

under the knee. It was no wonder she couldn't move.

The following hour passed without incident. 'I didn't see any point in panicking,' explains Mrs Sargent, 'as I thought someone was bound to come along eventually.' Wrapped up in her winter coat, with Zoe for added warmth and company, all she could do was to lie still in the freezing snow, and wait.

And wait she did, piecing together a possible rescue in her mind. She knew her neighbour normally checked in on Zoe at midday, and would raise the alarm then. But as the snow and the chill wind began to numb her senses, Mrs Sargent's thoughts turned to a heart attack she had suffered some 20 years before, and seeds of doubt began to set in. 'I couldn't help thinking about it,' she remembers, 'and it made me worry about how strong I really was.'

After a while, Mrs Sargent caught a glimpse of what she had been waiting for – help. At last! Another dog walker was coming towards her, further down the bridle path. It was only a matter of time before he reached her. She called out to him, but from her low position in the hedge she could not be seen. She called and called, but the wind whipped the words from her mouth, and stole her voice away. To compound her frustration, the walker turned back before reaching her. She continued to cry for help, but he soon disappeared from view.

Matters were more serious now. She was getting colder, and despite her cries, the whole world seemed to be ignoring her in her time of need. She was in great pain. She was freezing. And nobody was around to hear her.

Or at least, no human body.

The morning of the 21st of February was cold for everyone, man and beast. Mr Flynn arrived at his stables between 8 and 8.30am, and gave China his breakfast. And, as usual, he led his horse into the paddock while he mucked out and put down clean bedding for the day ahead. Because of the wintery conditions, there was no grazing to be had, so Errol also made sure he gave China some hay to feed on in the paddock.

> **'He kept flying up to me, and then charging off down the field, and galloping around the fence.'**

Normally, China would have eaten his breakfast quietly, and waited patiently to be saddled. But today, for some reason, the gelding was behaving strangely. 'To start with I just thought he had the wind up him,' recalls Errol. 'He kept flying up to me, and then charging off down the field, and galloping around the fence.'

Fifteen minutes later, Errol had finished mucking out. But China was still very agitated. After 18 years together, it didn't take much for Errol to realise that something was wrong. 'He looked at me,' explains Errol, 'then I looked at him, and then I followed him to the corner of the paddock.'

It wasn't long before Errol realised what had caught China's attention. From the far end of the paddock he could distinctly hear the distant cries of a woman. And by the sound of her, she was in some distress. 'I had, in fact, heard the cries earlier without realising what it was,' explains Errol. 'There's a military base nearby and we often get a lot of background noise from there.'

But now there was no doubt. In the poor conditions, Errol immediately realised the need for back-up. Luckily, farm owner Martin Knowles was close at hand on his tractor. Summoning his help, Errol lost no time in heading for the farm boundary. It was heavy going as the two men battled through the snow. Reaching the hedgerow separating the paddock from the bridleway beyond, they started to force their way through.

Hidden low-down in the hedge, Mrs Sargent was still unaware that help had almost arrived. Time and pain had fused into one. She had lost track of how long she had been waiting. Then she heard it. The familiar juddering noise of a tractor engine. 'I remember shouting: "Help! if you can hear me, I need help, please!"' she says.

Farm owner Martin Knowles swung into action on his tractor.

Errol fought his way through the hawthorn hedge to reach Mrs Sargent.

And this time her cries were heard. 'To my relief I heard this voice say: "It's okay! We know you're there. We're coming.",' she recalls. It was only seconds later that Errol and Martin burst through the hedgerow, and quickly clambered over the barbed wire fence separating them from their target. The wintry conditions had become even worse, and with a gale blowing it was evident that it just wasn't enough to have been found. Mary needed warmth, and urgently.

'When we found her she was conscious but she was in a bad way,' remembers Errol. 'She was white and freezing cold. Her lips were already going blue.' Fearing the onset of hypothermia, Errol used his mobile phone to call an ambulance, redirecting them a second time to the best access point for the bridleway. Luckily for Mrs Sargent, a second team was also contacted to assist in transporting her to safety.

It was only later that Mrs Sargent was told that her saviour was currently calmly eating hay in his paddock. 'There is no doubt about it,' says Errol, 'if China hadn't heard her cries and acted like he did, I would never have heard her.' Mrs Sargent certainly agrees. She puts it simply: 'He's a hero.'

Pet Casebook

Tasha the Sheep-Rottweiler

Beaten and left to starve, the story of Tasha, a nine-stone Rottweiler, is an inspirational tale of resilience and courage. Tasha, or Gnasha as she was called then, spent her puppyhood being trained to kill and maim small animals by her owner, a suspected drug addict. Kittens and rabbits regularly served as running live bait. Trusting and loyal, Gnasha carried out her cruel master's every command. She knew no other way.

Her owner soon grew tired of her. As the novelty of a large and fierce-looking dog wore off, Gnasha was left to fend for herself. Tired and hungry, she took to wandering the local streets in search of the odd meagre scrap of food. By the time Rottweiler Welfare picked her up, she was starving, dehydrated and scarred from severe beatings about the legs and hind quarters.

Gnasha was housed in a council dog pound for the statutory seven days. A local vet checked her over but didn't give her much chance of survival. A once magnificent beast, Gnasha was now little more than a pathetic bundle of skin, bone and bruises. Worse still, she was riddled with viruses and getting weaker by the minute. It was only a matter of time before she died or was destroyed to put her out of her misery.

Pet File

Pet name: Tasha.
Age: 4 ¹/₂ years.
Likes: Lying on her back with paws in the air; scoffing bacon and egg; other dogs.
Dislikes: Bars or any kind of railings.
Hobbies: Playing with rabbits on the farm.

The Rottweiler

Origins: Originally herding dogs, the Rottweiler was developed from Roman cattle dogs who would walk herds for miles and miles. Famous for their strong guarding instinct, Rottweilers were often used for the safe transfer of money in bags around their neck. The Rottweiler was named after the town of Rottweil in Wurttemberg, Southern Germany.
Height/weight: average 60cm/ 50 kg.
Characteristics:
● Massive, powerful body.
● High deterrent factor.
● Strong protective instincts.

Tasha with Anne in South Wales.

High on a mountain top in Wales, Anne and Rob Richards were busy on their farm near Neath. After a phone call from a friend, they offered to take the dog in, despite already having nine other dogs, including three Rottweilers. They knew the dog they had heard about over the phone had little chance of survival but they weren't deterred. 'We were told this dog was in care and desperately in need of a new home,' Rob recalls, 'and we just wanted to do everything we could to help.'

Within a few days, Gnasha was renamed Tasha and was on her way to South Wales. The night she arrived torrential rain lashed the hillsides, aided and abetted by an unforgiving wind. Inside the farmhouse, the clock ticked on relentlessly as Tasha's new owners paced the floorboards, awaiting their new arrival.

At midnight there was a knock at the door. Rescue worker Dave Williams stood in the doorway cradling Tasha in his arms. Anne and Rob wrapped the shivering animal in blankets and hot- water bottles and laid her down on the floor. The sight of her trembling frame reduced them both to tears.

The sight of her trembling frame reduced them both to tears.

'We knew she'd be bad but it was still shocking to see this poor creature who couldn't move or stand,' remembers Anne. 'She lay on the floor and we got down on our hands and knees to talk to her. We never thought she'd live she looked so pathetic.'

John Campbell, her new vet, explained that along with medication Tasha would need constant emotional support. The family would have to keep her spirits up and give her a new will to live. She had very little reason to struggle on, he explained, since she had only ever known cruelty and suffering.

Tasha had only known cruelty and suffering before she met the Richards.

It was a sleepless night for all concerned. 'We got her through by sitting up and talking to her,' Anne explains, 'and we gave her glucose solutions and other things – whatever we thought would give her a bit of energy.' Their efforts paid off. Tasha survived the night. But along with her other problems, the vet had also diagnosed Parvo virus, a killer gastric condition.

'He wanted to keep her in on a drip,' explains Rob. 'But I said that if she was going to die she should do so with her head on someone's lap.' So Rob and Anne agreed to take on Tasha's medical care themselves. It was

Above: Tasha is a surrogate mum to the young lambs.

Left: Tasha takes her job as a sheep-dog as seriously as any Collie.

a case of plain hard work. For the next four days Tasha needed to be fed with a syringe every 20 minutes, 24 hours a day. Despite the long haul ahead of them, Anne and Robert remained determined. They worked as a team. Anne would oversee feeding; Robert would encourage and stroke poor Tasha's head. A couple of days later, their efforts were rewarded. Shaking like a leaf, Tasha finally managed to stand up. Slowly the big dog gained energy, eating scrambled egg and rediscovering an appetite. But there was a long way to go: 'When we took her outside for the first time, she swayed from side to side,' explains Rob, 'but then a day later she tried to bag two chickens. That's when we knew she'd make it!'

Dog and farmer spent many hours together, Rob talking to Tasha, all the time quietly stroking her. Gradually, Tasha started to adapt to her new life. She learnt that she didn't need to kill for food any more and that not every human was a cruel abuser. Eventually, Rob and Tasha became almost inseparable as, miraculously, Tasha made a full recovery.

It was springtime, and the worst time of the year for Rob to lose one of his sheepdogs, a German Shepherd. With the lambing season beginning, being one dog down made all the difference. Rob decided that he had nothing to lose by trying out Tasha. 'I wasn't at all sure it would work,' he says. 'But I was wrong.'

Although most people would never associate a Rottweiler with farming, Tasha's natural instincts went back a long way. The Rottweiler breed came from Europe in Roman times and were used to herd cattle. Tasha quickly began to draw on behaviour that was literally printed in her genes. Soon it was obvious to all that she was a natural.

Rob was greatly impressed with Tasha's herding abilities but he also realised that with her gentle nature there was a far more specialised contribution she could make to the team: caring for new-born lambs.

Lambs must be born feet first if delivery is to be unaided. If the head appears first, both lamb and ewe are in a life-threatening situation, as the ewe, on experiencing the birth pangs, often runs from the

Rob is proud of his unconventional sheep-dog.

pain before collapsing out of sheer fright. This can often be fatal, particularly to the lamb, or if not fatal, it will often be maiming, as crows frequently peck at these defenceless young.

Time is of the essence in this situation, and Rob quickly found that with his new and highly able assistant, he could aid a successful birth within two minutes of first sight of the problem. 'A normal sheep-dog could do it,' explains Rob. 'It has a natural herding instinct after all. But with the ewe so distressed, it can often run straight past you and over the sheep-dog too. Tasha, on the other hand, can catch a ewe where a sheep-dog can't. She's got the speed, the weight and the strength.'

Last year Tasha saved about 30 lambs. Now every lambing season sees her using her own unique skills to help ewes that are suffering breech births. And that's not all. Despite her cruel start in life, Tasha has a gentle caring way with the new-borns. After suffering a bad birth, many ewes do not bond with their new lambs, often walking off in disinterest. Once again, Tasha comes to the rescue by inspecting these new-born orphans and 'washing' them, awakening the maternal instinct in the ewes, she reunites them with their young.

'She may have forgiven, but she hasn't forgotten.'

These days, Tasha is a fully-fledged member of the Richards' team of working dogs. Despite human oppression early in her life that trained her to kill and maim, she has reverted to what comes naturally to her – nurturing (a trait that does not come easily to a herding sheep-dog).

Her unique skills have already brought her recognition. Tasha is well known locally not only for her sheep caring but also as a canine personality who appears at many different charity events. She visits local infant schools where the children love her. Even the inmates of the local prison are great fans and made a special poster board for her. She has also been the recipient of several national titles.

Seeing his pride and joy running across the mountainside taking care of her charges, Rob is still in awe of Tasha's resilience. But, as he explains, 'She may have forgiven but she hasn't forgotten. She's always got that far away look in her eyes.'

Anne is just as proud of Tasha's achievements. 'She's saved the life of so many lambs,' she explains. 'And she gives back so much joy and love. Much more than she's ever received. Much more than we could every repay.'

Pet Casebook

Smokey the Listening Cat

MANY OF THE REMARKABLE ANIMALS FEATURED IN 'PET POWER' HAVE ACTED purely on their natural instincts. Others have honed their inherent talents through constant training and attention. In the case of Smokey the cat, pure instinct has been developed into a set of astonishing abilities. And the most surprising thing of all is the fact that this particular training course was designed by Smokey herself without any outside aid.

A pedigree Russian Blue now enjoying the autumn of her years, Smokey has been living with the Nabarro family since she was six weeks old. Mary and Philip Nabarro live in Torquay with their daughter Jane, who has her own flat around the corner. They are a close-knit, loving and contented family. They also all have substantial hearing difficulties, to differing degrees, and mostly communicate by a combination of sign language and lip-reading.

Jane was 16 years old when her parents brought home their new cat Smokey for the first time. Mary and Philip were determined to select a green-eyed Russian Blue from a breeder they had been told about in Wales. So despite a heavy snowstorm and a severe detour caused by the closure of the Severn Bridge, the Nabarros kept driving, and finally returned triumphantly to Torquay, with, as Mary remembers it, 'this tiny fluffy thing in the back'.

At the time, Jane was away from the area, studying at a school for the hard of hearing. When she returned home for the holidays, Smokey was there waiting for her. It didn't take long for cat and family to build up an

Mary, Jane and Philip Nabarro with Smokey at the Arthur Acatemy Awards.

extraordinary rapport. 'We used to be dog lovers, really,' explains Philip, 'but that all changed when we met Smokey.'

When Smokey was 18 months old, the Nabarros began to notice some unusual behaviour. Unusual, at least, for a cat. Known more for their independent spirit than their demands for attention, most cats use very different and less direct communication signals than their canine counterparts. Nevertheless, Smokey appeared to be making a point of sitting in front of members of the family when she wanted her wishes known.

But in this particular family, communication between pet and owners had to develop in a very special way. As a result of their individual hearing difficulties, the Nabarros spend most of their time communicating with each other using sign language. It evidently did not take Smokey very long to realise that her owners were special in this regard.

But it didn't stop there. With this knowledge in mind, Smokey began to communicate with her owners on a daily basis, aware that they were unable to

Pet File

Name: Smokey.
Age: 13 years.
Breed: Pedigree Russian Blue.
Likes: Mellowing out in the sun, avocado, marshmallow.

Dislikes: Having to go outside in anything but sunshine.
Hobbies: Sleeping; riding along in the car.

hear noises in and around the flat themselves. She would alert them to the doorbell, to the phone, to the presence of a prowler in the garden. With no formal training, Smokey had quickly become the family's ears. In fact, between the ages of $1\frac{1}{2}$ through to 12, Smokey has been the Nabarro's very own, self-taught hearing cat.

But it isn't just the everyday family activities and tasks that Smokey helps with. Her vigilance and sensitivity has averted the odd minor disaster as well. 'My parents were away for the weekend,' remembers Jane, 'and I was by myself in my flat. I'd been washing up and inadvertently left the taps running.'

Jane moved through to the living room and began to watch TV. But after ten minutes, she noticed that Smokey was pacing up and down in front of her, trying to attract her attention. 'When I finally realised that Smokey was trying to tell me something,' continues Jane, 'I followed her back into the kitchen, where the water was overflowing. I couldn't hear it!'

Smokey's unique brand of feline intelligence came into its own, however,

Jane is proud of Smokey's special achievements.

when Jane went to college in London. Renting a flat in South London, she took Smokey along with her to keep her company while she studied for her English Literature degree and indeed keep her safe at the same time. It wasn't long before Smokey proved her worth once more when another aquatic disaster struck:

'It was late in the evening, and again, I was sitting watching TV when Smokey sat in front of me and wouldn't leave me alone,' Jane explains. 'So I followed her to the kitchen, where the top of the taps had come off! It was literally flooding the place out. I had to put her in the bathroom, I was so worried that she'd drown.'

But Smokey isn't just able to recognise impending domestic disasters. Another incident illustrates just how acute her perception of the world was on behalf of her beloved Jane. It was 10 pm, and Jane had been studying hard at college once more. She had arrived home to be welcomed, as usual, by Smokey. Jane's evening routine was quite straightforward: she would feed her cat, read the papers, cook herself some dinner and relax in front of the television.

HAPPY VALENTINES DAY

Smokey certainly doesn't get left out on Valentine's Day.

To our wonderful cat Smokey,

Lots of love and purrs from

Mary, Philip and Mistress Jane — and the cat gang at Lydwell Park Road

'It was getting quite late,' she remembers. 'When Smokey suddenly came over from the window right up to me. She didn't look very happy either.' A slight incident, but Smokey's actions set off alarm bells in Jane's head. Worried, she approached the window and it was then that she saw him. An unfamiliar man was standing outside and staring in. For a woman living alone in a big city it was an unsettling moment: 'I phoned my boyfriend,' Jane recalls, 'and he came round and managed to get him to go away.' Once again, Smokey's early warning system had proved effective in preventing small events turning into possible serious ones.

These days, age 13 plus, Smokey is taking life a bit more easily. A confirmed home-lover, she prefers a night on the sofa to a night on the roof tiles. But even off-duty at home, she's still as alert as ever, an uncomplaining information service; listening, waiting and watching over her family.

CAT FACTS

- The reason cats' eyes shine in the dark is because of tapetum, a reflective layer in the eye, which acts like a mirror.
- The oldest cat on record was probably 'Puss', a tabby owned by Mrs Holway of Clayhidon, Devon. Puss passed on in 1939, having celebrated his 36th birthday.
- Did you know more than 10,000 cats are 'employed' by the British Government to keep official buildings free from rodents?
- In five years, a female cat can be responsible for up to 20,000 descendants.
- According to experts, sun-seeking cats need to watch out as much as humans for over-exposure to UV rays. They suggest keeping your moggie in the shade or putting a high factor sun block on the tips of its ears and nose.

That Loving Feline

Scientific studies have shown that watching your cat's tail is the key to understanding its feelings. Pay close attention to the rear end of your furry friend and you might spot these four common positions:

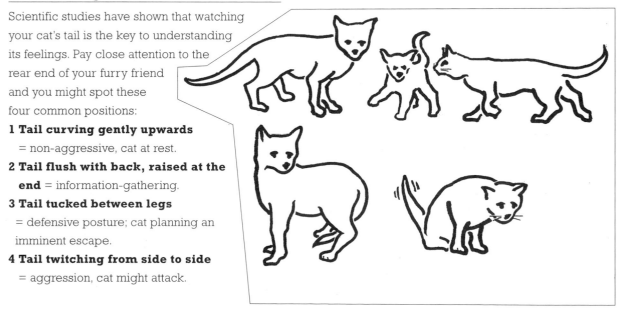

1 **Tail curving gently upwards** = non-aggressive, cat at rest.
2 **Tail flush with back, raised at the end** = information-gathering.
3 **Tail tucked between legs** = defensive posture; cat planning an imminent escape.
4 **Tail twitching from side to side** = aggression, cat might attack.

Pet Casebook

Wellard the Cheeky Cockerel

SCHOOL PROJECTS CAN BE DANGEROUS THINGS. TEST TUBES CAN BREAK, nature trails can turn muddy, colour photocopies can blur. Many innocent experiments can result in the creation of something truly monstrous. But for one particular school in Newchurch, on the Isle of Wight, one class project was responsible for more than its fair share of destruction. Perhaps the incubator was too hot. Perhaps a dose of radiation leaked in from a digital watch. No one can be sure. But one thing is certain: after their project was completed, the world was a more dangerous place. For it was from this school that Wellard the cockerel was hatched.

You might think the hatching of a cockerel does not merit much attention. But sometimes, from little acorns, enormously assertive chickens can grow. Indeed, as soon as he erupted from that egg, there was no doubting that this was no ordinary chicken. He was strong, single-minded and fearless. In fact, he was Wellard.

Pam's relationship with Wellard is a privileged one.

GEORGE GALE & CO
POINTER INN

HOME OF WELLARD
GOOD HOMECOOKED
FOOD
NO CHICKEN!

Top: Wellard likes the odd tipple.

Above: Beware of the cockerel – Wellard has become a fixture at the pub.

Wellard the cockerel wasted no time in making his mark on the world. His first step on his path to destruction was to dig up as many flowerbeds as possible. He had soon become such a nuisance that the school had no choice but to get rid of him.

The first encumbent owner was a man called Paul, a pub entertainer who lived in a flat. He had taken the cockerel in as an act of good faith, but it was soon clear that there was no love lost between man and chicken. At least, this particular chicken. Wellard was on the move again.

This time, his luck was in. Ray Steele and Pam White are business partners who run the Pointer Inn in Newchurch, and are friends of Paul and his partner Sharon. At this time, Ray and Pam were running a pub called The Sun, and because they already had a few chickens in the back garden, they saw it in their hearts to take him on.

Settling in for a cockerel like Wellard wasn't easy. 'The other cockerel kept him away from the chickens we had then,' explains Ray, 'so he was a bit frustrated.' Maybe it was frustration. Maybe it was simply a bad attitude. But

Pet File

Pet name: Wellard.

Age: Unknown.

Likes: Lying on his back with legs in the air; his favourite shawl; bacon rinds, fat off ham and lettuce.

Dislikes: The pub gardener; certain regulars.

Hobbies: Having mud baths; pecking Scruffy the dog on his backside for no apparent reason.

Wellard's behaviour did not improve with time. 'He used to go round to the front door and if we didn't let him in he'd leave an unwelcome present on the doorstep,' remembers Pam. 'Then he'd walk off to terrorise people waiting at the bus stop.'

Another Wellard activity of note during this period was posing as an unofficial car park attendant. This was where he would walk up to cars in the car park and simply stand and stare. Customers would be trapped inside their cars, too terrified to get out.

But Wellard's lively temperament also had its advantages. 'He used to, and still does, chase sales reps away,' smiles Pam. 'I remember there was one who ended up holding up her briefcase to fend him off.'

When Ray and Pam moved into the Pointer Inn, Wellard had established a pattern of behaviour that was not going to be broken. He has free run of the Pointer Inn, and can come and go as he pleases. Indeed, he is one of the few chickens in Britain who can claim to be a resident feature of a public house.

The Pointer Inn is a village pub, benefitting from a sizeable local trade even without holiday makers. Wellard lives in the large back garden, sharing his living space with a sheep called Maggie. There are also three dogs, Charlie, Libby and Scruffy, and two cats, Sid and Jaffa. The cats seem to know best, and keep out of Wellard's way. Sometimes the dogs aren't so lucky ...

Luck is also something that features heavily in Wellard's life. When he first moved in with Ray and Pam, their other cockerel took an instant dislike to him and would attack him on sight. Once, he took Wellard by surprise and knocked the wind out of him. 'We shut him in a special little hen house to recover,' recalls Pam. 'That night, the fox got the other cockerel and all the chickens. Wellard was okay because he was shut in the hen house.'

Gleefully indifferent to his own good fortune, Wellard spends his days ensuring that most people understand who's boss. Locals have been known to tremble when Pam shouts those immortal words, 'Wellard's out everyone!' As he struts around, king cockerel of all he surveys, everyone is truly on their best behaviour.

Like most pub locals, he has his own place at the bar and drinks from his own pint glass of beer. After knocking back a fine draught, he might wander over to the beer garden, jump on a table and pinch a few sandwiches from an unsuspecting punter's lunch. 'I often have to replace customers sandwiches,' muses Ray. 'He sometimes does this side shuffle and swipes them out of their hands.'

After a stout lunch, Wellard likes nothing better than harassing delivery men who might make the huge mistake of actually trying to deliver something. 'He's been after our barrel delivery man recently,' says Pat. 'I think the man was new, so he wasn't expecting anything. He should have read the sign: 'Pointer Inn – Home of Wellard!'.

The cats seem to know best, and keep out of Wellard's way.

But a cockerel can't spend a whole afternoon worrying delivery men. There's always Norman to consider. Norman is the gardener, and probably qualifies as the most long-suffering of Wellard's many victims. 'He'll sweep up the leaves, and then Wellard will just jump into them and shoo them all over the place,' says Ray. 'Norman gets furious if he's trying to fix the lawnmower and Wellard is hanging around, provoking him!'

But it's not all hard work for Wellard. The softer side of this cocky cockerel is only on show to those who know him well. 'He loves being wrapped up in a shawl and having his tummy tickled,' says Pam's 15-year-old daughter Elvisa. 'He's a softie really.'

Some softie. Energised by his late afternoon shawl session, Wellard's evening is usually filled with more bullying, interspersed with various vain attempts to woo the handbags of the female clientele. 'He's got this real liking for handbags,' explains Ray. 'He tends to get a bit amorous. Maybe he just likes the look of them.'

Opinion is divided on just how useful it is to have a sociopathic cockerel roaming around on a Friday night. Some locals love him, some would rather he was served up in a basket for Sunday lunch. But the canniest reason of all comes from Ray: 'He's good for business, really. We've had customers racing in the door, because he chases them in.'

For Ray and Pam, it seems, keeping hold of their renegade pub pet isn't a hard decision at all. Wellard is far from being barred.

TV Reconstruction

Tess and the Rockpool

IT WAS A QUIET MORNING IN THE OPERATIONS ROOM OF SWANSEA COAST-guard station, but when watch officer Graham Martin saw the incident report screen, he knew the peace was about to end. Officer Bernice Martin had taken the call ... a child in a rockpool ... a dog pulling him out. Within seconds, a team of coastguards had been despatched. Incident no. 860 sounded serious.

The events that led to this call had started many hours earlier on a beach in South Wales. Those involved would never forget.

The wide sandy beach at Broughton on the Gower Peninsula in South Wales was the perfect place for a family day out. In this case, the family were the Whines: Cherie, her husband Dean, and their three-year-old son Arron. Cherie's brother Clive was also with them, with his wife Mo and their son Wayne. The Whines had come down to visit Clive for the day, and were looking forward to a fun-packed afternoon, relaxing by the sea. They arrived at the beach around 11.30 am, and as it was a little breezy, set up their windbreakers beside a small cove.

The cove was only a tiny distance away from a large rockpool, one of the Whines's

Dean, Arron and Cherie Whines.

Pet File

Name: Tess.

Age: 13 years.

Likes: Apples; titbits, especially chocolate drops; swimming in the sea or in any form of water (she once jumped into a swimming pool on holiday and also dived into a neighbour's pond!).

Dislikes: Fireworks.

Hobbies: Giving people 'The Look' when she doesn't want to do something; taking up as much room as possible along with fellow housemate Tammy (a Retriever) on Heather's new sofa.

The Labrador Retriever

Origins: A strongly built dog, the Labrador Retriever is one of Britain's most popular dog breeds. Originating in Newfoundland, the Labrador was first used as a fisherman's aid. Its job was to swim to shore carrying the ends of fishing nets.

Height/weight: average 55cm/average 28 kg.

Characteristics:

- Home-loving, this breed's friendly, affectionate nature makes it ideal for children.

Heather Hodder and Tess.

- A good obedience dog, the Labrador is frequently used by the police and armed services.
- Loves water and cool temperatures

favourite spots on the beach: 'It's quite big, and was pretty deep that day,' says Cherie. 'It was a nice little pool for the kids to swim in.' Depending on the time of year and the tides, the pool could vary from a broad, deep body of water to a dry sandbank. On the 30th June, 1991, there was enough water to fill the pool to a depth of almost 2 metres.

Not surprisingly, young Arron was keen to check on his favourite spot. A quick tour was provided by his Dad, Dean. 'I saw little Arron go with his Dad and Uncle; they were only going a few feet to the rocks,' remembers Cherie. 'I wasn't worried as long as he was with them.' It was his Dad who dropped him back at the windbreak. 'I sent him back to his Mam,' says Dean, 'and the last I saw of him, he was only a few feet from her and the others.'

With innocent enthusiasm, Arron began to climb.

The two men then began to climb to the top in order to look at the nearby race track through their binoculars. At the bottom of the rocks, Arron turned to see his father and Uncle Clive ascending the craggy rockface. It looked like fun. Perhaps he'd give it a go. With innocent enthusiasm, Arron put a tiny foot on the base of the rock, steadied himself with his hand, and began to climb.

Unknown to Arron, his fate lay in the hands of a young member of another family. For the Whines were not alone on the beach that day.

Every summer, Heather Hodder and her husband Steve travel down to Whitford Bay Campsite near Broughton Beach, to stay in their caravan. Tess, their black Labrador, is always keen to come too, because it means she can enjoy two of the best things in doggy life – running along the beach, and fetching sticks from the rockpool.

On this particular June day, Heather and her brother Philip had come down to the campsite, and were out on their regular walk with Tess. They were taking a path that took them across the top of the bay, before heading down a sandy bank that led to the seashore. As usual, Tess was off the lead, and, as usual, she was dashing to and fro some distance ahead, exploring and taking in the sea air.

As Heather approached the area with the rockpool, she noticed that Tess's movements had become less erratic, and that instead of following whatever scent took her fancy, she was running full pelt towards the rockpool. Naturally, Heather assumed her dog was keen to start their usual game of 'fetching sticks from the water'. Heather was sorry she had forgotten to pick some up on her way down the bank. As Tess increased her speed across the beach, Heather wondered what might be holding her attention. She and her brother quickened their pace in pursuit.

On top of the rocks, Dean and Clive had also noticed the sprinting dog. 'Look at that,' said Clive. 'Wonder where he's off to?' The two men watched with interest as Tess sprang from the edge of the rockpool, and into the water. Perhaps the dog was retrieving a stick.

Back on the beach, Heather and her brother watched as their dog struggled in the water. Tess was dragging something to the side of the pool with her mouth. 'She was doing doggie paddle, trying to push it out of the water,' remembers Heather. 'My brother and I both thought it was an umbrella when we first saw it. As we got closer, and she brought it right to the edge, I said, "it's a child!"'

Hearing the cry from below, Dean looked again at the dog in the water. But something else caught his eye. Something that made his stomach churn. It was the green sleeve of a jacket. A very familiar jacket. Now there was no doubt. It was Arron.

The two brothers scrambled down the rocks. By the side of the pool, Arron was lying motionless, his lips already turning blue. Recalling a first aid programme, Clive turned the little boy over and began rubbing his back.

Cherie was already running: 'I tried to get to them so fast,' she recalls. 'I just ran straight across the pool, and I was soaked. It must have been three feet deep, but I didn't care; I tried to walk on water to get to Arron.'

Meanwhile, Clive was doing his utmost to give the kiss of life to his nephew. Minutes later his efforts paid off as Arron's lungs spluttered back into life. Unbeknown to Clive, help was already on its way. A runner on the beach had witnessed the commotion and had run to nearby Broughton Farm Caravan Park. Site co-owner Robert Elson and houseguest Dr David Bullpitt were shocked to hear the news. Leaving Mrs Elson to phone the coastguard, the two men jumped into their Land Rover and sped off. 'We should have taken the

Caravan park site co-owner Robert Elson.

tractor on that beach,' explains Robert, 'but there just wasn't time. We raced across the sand at about 60 miles an hour. Luckily when we got to the scene, the child had already been revived by his uncle.'

When Dr Bullpitt first arrived beside Arron, his face was grave. 'I'm not sure if it was lack of oxygen or cold, but he was completely purple,' he remembers now. Dr Bullpitt decided it was important to move Arron back to

RECONSTRUCTION

Right: Tess leapt into action.

Bottom left: She plunged into the rockpool ...

Bottom right: ... and dragged Arron to safety.

the shelter of Robert's house. Carefully, the men lifted Arron into the back of the Land Rover, where Dean and Cherie held their son tight. Back in the kitchen of the farmhouse, Dr Bullpitt placed Arron in the recovery position. Thankfully, it was only a matter of minutes before the ambulance services arrived.

'Luckily the annual Gower bike ride was taking place that weekend,' explains Robert Elson, 'which meant that the emergency services were all on standby.' With the help of a police escort, Arron was taken to Singleton Hospital, and has since made a full recovery.

In hindsight, such a horrific experience brings both chaos and complication. But everyone is agreed that there was one witness who remained calm throughout this terrible ordeal: Tess. 'I'm not a spiritual person,' explains Clive, 'but that dog knew what it had done, and wouldn't leave Arron's side till he was better.'

A few years older now, Tess doesn't leap into the water like she used to. But young Arron has done more than come to terms with his ordeal. He's joined a swimming club. 'I can't remember everything that happened,' he says. 'But I think that Tess is definitely a great dog.'

Tess received praise for her brave actions from everyone, including Arron.

THE CANINE COUNTDOWN

Straight in at no.1 as the UK's most popular breed of dog comes the German Shepherd. Next up is the Labrador, followed by Yorkshire Terriers, Spaniels and Jack Russells.

Pet Casebook

Popeye the Psychoparrot

O WNING A PET CAN SOMETIMES BE STRESSFUL. BUT THE PRESSURES EXERTED by one particular parrot on a marriage in Hastings, Sussex are bordering on the critical. The marriage in question is between Charles and Sally Coxsedge, and is 15 years old. The parrot in question is called Popeye, and is 3 ¹/₄ years old. He's a small Maximillian Pionus about the size of a pigeon, and he has made up his mind. No question about it. He's in love with Charles.

If you love someone ... preen their glasses.

Whenever Charles enters the room, Popeye makes his way onto his shoulder. After a few minutes of perching, he will take it upon himself to preen his beloved, or perhaps bow down his head in order to receive a gentle stroke behind the neck. In almost every respect, young Popeye behaves like a love-struck teenager when Charles is around. But with Sally, it's quite another story.

While his love for Charles has grown over the years, so Popeye has developed an equally focused, and no less intense, feeling for Sally: hatred. It is a truly spiteful, resentful, antagonistic hatred that goes beyond instinct and most of the laws of the jungle.

These extraordinary feelings of Popeye's are at their most strident when Sally is left alone with him. Once Charles has

Pet File

Name: Popeye.

Age: 3 ¼ years.

Breed: Maximillian Pionus.

Likes: Mr Charles Coxsedge; crisps, chips, tomatoes (as long as they're from Charles); having his head stroked.

Dislikes: Mrs Sally Coxsedge.

Habits: Talking; shouting; screaming; harassing Harvey the Rottweiler; removing Charles' glasses; pulling at his sideburns; outstaring anyone who dares to challenge his authority.

Most likely to say: 'Popeye's a good boy, give us a stroke!'

Least likely to say: 'I love you Sally, let me take you away from all this.'

Biggest moment: The day he escaped and flew next door: his big adventure.

gone to work, and the children are at school, Popeye's malevolent nature takes hold. High on his list of worrying tactics is divebombing, flying as close as he can to Sally without hitting her. 'He sometimes throws in a victory roll,' Sally explains, 'just to spite me.' If the two of them are in the same room, Sally will spend most of that time ducking him. But as she puts it herself, 'you can't spend a marriage ducking a bird.'

Charles is stoic about his pet's preferences. 'Basically what happens with parrots is that they start to form strong relationships with their keepers,' he explains. 'With me, I think he started to regard me as a mate.'

When he isn't divebombing Sally, Popeye will spend most of his time ignoring her, unless she comes close. Even if she is offering food, Popeye will either peck at her fingers or ignore her completely. Once, as a peace offering, Sally approached his perch holding half a tomato, one of his favourite foods.

'He just turned his back on me and muttered, "what do you want?",' remembers Sally. 'I couldn't believe it.'

Popeye's premeditated strikes against Sally seem to go against most accepted explanations of parrot behaviour. 'In the textbooks they say that parrots are basically shy creatures, and will not attack unless directly threatened,' explains Charles. 'But where Sally's concerned, he just goes looking for trouble.'

The only time Popeye controls his feelings, it seems, is when his loved one returns home. Although he remains protective of his beau, Popeye tends to mellow when perched on the shoulder of his significant other. But, as if it wasn't enough, Popeye is so jealous of Sally that he will use any means at his disposal to come between Charles and his human partner. In particular, he will take Charles's side in arguments. 'If we're trying to discuss something,' says Sally, 'he'll just start chiming in with whistles and squawks, shouting me down as much as he can.'

Three's too many, it seems, for a marriage. Especially if one of them has a beak. But it wasn't always like this. There was a happier time for Charles, Sally and Popeye. In the beginning, Popeye was a contented and amenable parrot. He even sung on the way home in the car when Charles and Sally bought him. 'He was happy as can be as we were driving him back,' remembers Sally. 'He was cooing and singing, and wolf-whistling at passers-by.'

For three weeks, he was a pet with perfect manners, being equally pleasant to both Charles and to Sally. But then, gradually, he began to shift allegiances over to Charles; and once he'd made up his mind, there was no going back. And the tensions and problems his attitude is creating are straining the bonds of matrimony. Sally is fed up of trying to be pleasant to this highly unfriendly bird. 'I decided it was either the bird, or me', she says.

Top: a disaster waiting to happen.

Above: Popeye ensures his presence is felt, even at meal times.

Popeye is hopelessly devoted to Charles.

But the 'Pet Power' team was convinced that there must be a way for harmony to prevail once more in the Coxsedge household. Rather than selling Popeye, they suggested that the couple gave peace just one more chance. The series drafted in a parrot behaviourist to help the Coxsedges relate to their bird in a more positive way, and perhaps even go so far as to reconcile Sally and Popeye. Irene Christie has been training and studying parrots, and parrot psychology, for many years. In fact, her stunning Macaw, Max, once featured in the James Bond film *For Your Eyes Only*.

'I've often been given misbehaving parrots to deal with,' Irene explains, 'and those I do take will usually be very well behaved with me. But to get full results you need to have the owners work it through in the home.' Through experience, Irene has learnt that many parrots act like belligerent teenagers and should be treated just the same. 'A lot of their bad behaviour is basically attention seeking, and the key, with parrots and teenagers alike, is to grit your teeth and keep going. It's better to get bitten than to back off.'

Irene made an expert analysis of the Coxsedge's situation and came up

Parrots act like belligerent teenagers and should be treated the same.

with a series of measures that would help bring Sally and Popeye to, if not a friendship, then hopefully, a more peaceful understanding.

First on her list was disorientation. By changing his surroundings, explained Irene, such as moving him to another room, Popeye would be more receptive to new ideas. The second stage was isolation. Popeye would not be allowed to see or have any other contact with his loved one for at least two weeks. During this period, Sally would have to feed him exclusively.

An important factor during all of this was status. In particular, the height of the cage or perch. In the wild, the bossiest and most dominant birds occupy the highest branches. 'Putting Popeye's cage in a lower position is a good start,' explains Irene, 'so that instead of looking down at you from their privileged position, they are looking up at the top bird. Shoulder-perching should be a

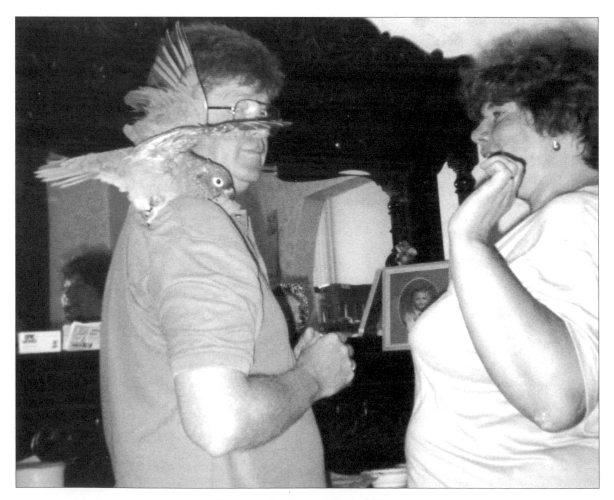

Popeye makes his preferences clear.

treat, reserved only for special occasions and extremely well-behaved birds.'

After the initial period of isolation, reinforced by a changed status, many birds begin to make minor advances towards their new parent. They might even start trying to reach out, and relate for the first time. In this event, Sally was told, she must avoid all references to the previous bad image. For Sally, this meant no cushions to protect her from Popeye's beak. No nerves. Only a smile and a steady hand. And, of course, Sally was also told to try to relate back; to spend time; perhaps even to learn to love.

Irene remains realistic about the long-term chances for success. 'In the end, parrots do sometimes just make up their mind,' she explains. 'You cannot make a parrot like you. There may be memories reinforced at an early age, with a previous owner. Or it could be something very minor, such as the bird missing a frequent visitor to the previous owner's house. This is why it is immensely important to get to know everything you can about your parrot before it moves in.'

Sally and Charles Coxsedge have tried their best with Popeye. It's now down to all three of them to work something out together. As in human relationships, sometimes you have to take things apart before you can put them back together.

A Parrot Therapy Checklist

When you are trying to make your misbehaving parrot treat you with politeness and a little more respect, there are many things you need to remember. Parrot psychologist Irene Christie has pinpointed seven major areas to bear in mind:

1 Disorientation. Be sure you take the bird out of its normal surroundings.

2 Isolation. Ensure the preferred partner does not come into contact with the bird.

3 Status. Adjust the position of the bird's cage so it knows who's in charge.

4 Reciprocation. If the bird begins to make advances towards you, ensure you return the compliment.

5 Towel control. Many parrots are hole-nesters and associate darkness with calm, and home, so throwing a towel over a cage may help it to relax if it gets agitated.

6 Spending time with your pet. Most important of all. In order for a parrot to like you, they must first get to know you.

7 Acknowledging defeat. It's worth remembering that even if you do try your hardest, it may just be that the parrot has made up its mind. In this case, you must simply accept that there may be nothing you can do. You can get a parrot to tolerate you, but getting it to like you is a wholly different kettle of feathers.

THAT'S THE WAY I LIKE IT
African Greys are the only parrots who prefer their human owners to be of the opposite sex!

TV Reconstruction

Taff's Fire Mission

Yvonne Bartlett lives in a small cottage near Matlock, Derbyshire. Together with her daughter Julie, she runs a successful riding centre and school on the premises. Like many such establishments, the Bartletts have several working animals including three Border Collies: Taff, Chad and Millie.

Working with other animals around, it was important that the dogs were taught to be obedient to their owners. For Yvonne, this also meant setting out the rules of the house. 'We made it quite clear to all three of our dogs that they weren't allowed upstairs,' she explains. 'They slept in the lounge, and it was adults only upstairs.'

Taff, Yvonne's favourite, was a hit from the start. A wonderfully tempered dog, he proved an old hand at rounding up stray horses, his Collie instincts serving him well. All he needed to hear was one shout of 'fetch!' and he would zoom into action. But Yvonne never realised that Taff's sharp intelligence and initiative would have far more important uses in the very near future.

It was 11 pm on a cold January night in 1992. True to routine, Yvonne went out to check on the horses in their stables. Reassured, she returned to her cottage, flushed from the winter air. She chatted over a cup of tea with Julie and her boyfriend John. 'When you've been outside in the fresh air all day,' says Yvonne, 'the heat inside makes you feel like going to sleep.' It wasn't very long before humans and canines alike were tucked up in bed.

In the front room, Taff, Chad and Millie were curled up in their usual spot in front of the fire. They often slept there, its glowing embers providing welcome warmth after a hard day's work. Familiar with the well-worn household rituals, they little expected to be woken before first light. But a few hours later something unexpected happened.

Instead of dying away, the fire crackled, spitting an ember out onto the floor. As the Collies rose, their sleep disrupted, the spark turned into a flame. A small fire quickly gathered momentum.

Many dogs instinctively recognise when unusual events are taking place and the Bartlett dogs were no different. But though instinct told the trio something was badly wrong, what to do was another matter. Their training was very specific: roaming around was frowned upon, and upstairs was definitely out-of-bounds.

The fire was taking hold. Sofas, walls, carpets ... each fell victim one by

Yvonne and Taff.

Pet File

Pet name: Taff.

Age: 7 years.

Likes: Regular morning biscuit when Yvonne has her tea; fuss and petting in the mornings.

Dislikes: Fuss and petting in the evenings; loud noises.

Hobbies: Playing with his huge squeaky dummy!; carrying buckets at play with son Chad.

The Border Collie

Origins: The Border Collie originated centuries ago in the border country between England and Scotland and was primarily a sheep herding dog.

Height/weight: about 47cm at shoulder/average 20 kg.

Characteristics:
- Highly intelligent.
- Obedient and easy to train.
- Good companion.
- Great family pet, good with children.

one to the hungry line of flames. Burning wallpaper began to flake off and float around the room, and on the ceiling, a black veil of smoke was creeping down the walls and choking out the light. As the temperature rose, the dogs edged into the hallway. Perhaps their mistress would come down and help them there. But on the floor above, no one stirred.

Yvonne, Julie and John were still in the depths of sleep. What's more, without outside intervention, they were unlikely to wake up. The thick black smoke was pouring from the front room, and drifting upwards to the bedrooms. An unseen and deadly killer, it was enveloping everything in its wake.

The Collies continued to wait anxiously at the foot of the stairs. It's not always in an animal's nature to wake an owner in a fire. Dogs faced with similar situations have been known to go and hide, their instinct for self-preservation coming to the fore. Luckily for the Bartlett household, one of their dogs was less selfish (and less law-abiding) than they had imagined.

For it was at this point that Taff chose to make the most intelligent – and disobedient – move of his life. While Chad and Millie cowered in a corner, Taff scampered towards the door with one aim: to find his mistress, no matter what the consequences.

He pawed at the door to the stairs and, finding a gap, finished the job with his muzzle. The stairwell was choked with smoke, but Taff negotiated the steep steps without difficulty. The next obstacle was Yvonne's sliding bedroom door. This was another matter. Taff pushed at it repeatedly with his nose but to no avail. Finally, with the smoke stinging his eyes, he scratched for a final time, and was rewarded when it slid open. He was there!

The first thing Yvonne was aware of was a heavy weight landing with a thud on her bed. 'I just woke up and put the light on,' she recalls. 'I saw all this smoke and I thought: fire.' She leapt out of bed, and moved to her door. Sliding it back she suddenly felt a blast of heat from the fire below. Moving along the corridor, she began calling for Julie and John. Then, barefoot and pyjama-clad she descended the burning stairs.

He pawed at the door to the stairs and, finding a gap, finished the job with his muzzle.

'I was horrified,' Yvonne recalls. 'Flames were up all the stairs and the front room was covered with fire. Two of the dogs were sat at the bottom of the stairs, probably waiting for me to let them out!' Disorientated and frightened, Yvonne focused all her energy on getting out with the two other dogs through the kitchen door. 'I didn't really think about the danger at all at that point,' she remembers. 'I just thought I must get everybody else outside.'

Alerted by Yvonne's cries, Julie and John quickly pulled on some clothes, but when they opened their bedroom door a wall of smoke confronted them. In an effort to try to reduce the damage to the house, John decided to shut the upstairs doors. He closed the door to their bedroom, and slid Yvonne's door tightly shut. But as he slammed the bathroom door, he didn't realise there was one important occupant who was hidden from view. Taking cover from the dense smoke, Taff had wandered into the bathroom and curled up on the floor. Unwittingly, John had locked in the family's rescuer.

Outside, John and Julie joined Yvonne, coughing and shaken, but alive. Collecting her distracted thoughts, Yvonne turned to her beloved dogs. One, two ... but where was Taff? Julie remembers the moment well. 'Mum knew that the dog was inside and she knew it had saved us and that it might die.'

A neighbour called the fire brigade as John used fire extinguishers and a stable hose to try and do something, anything, to quell the flames.

RECONSTRUCTION ■ ■ ■ ■ ■ ■ ■ ■ ■ ■ ■ ■ ■ ■ ■ ■

Taff had to open Yvonne's bedroom door.

He roused Yvonne from a deep sleep.

Yvonne, coughing and shaken, but alive, her distracted thoughts turned to her beloved dogs.

Fire officer Chris Gregory was met by a distressed Yvonne. 'When we got there, everybody was already out,' he explains. 'But the dog was still in the house. Obviously they were all very concerned about the dog and we were asked to go and find Taff.'

Chris put on his breathing apparatus and braved the flames. But in the thick smoke, the lay-out of the house was difficult to fathom. Climbing the stairs he could barely see or hear anything. It was not going to be easy finding a dog in those kind of conditions.

RECONSTRUCTION ■ ■ ■ ■ ■ ■ ■

Taff was saved by fire officer Chris Gregory.

But when he opened the bathroom door and crouched on his hands and knees he found the unconscious form he was looking for. Taff's breathing was shallow and he was soaking wet with sweat. 'He was one of the heaviest things I have ever lifted,' remembers Chris. 'I managed to get him into my arms and struggle back through the smoke to get outside. When I laid him out on the grass we all thought he was dead.'

The family were horrified. 'We thought it was too late,' Julie remembers. 'We really thought that Taff had had it.' It seemed unthinkable that Taff's brave actions should have such a tragic end. But as the fresh air hit the Collie's lungs, Taff came round with a wheeze and a cough. Relief poured over everyone present. He was going to be all right.

To keep Taff warm, Yvonne took him to the stables. By the time the vet arrived, there was little to do save check him over.

The Bartlett family are under no doubts as to the real hero of the night. Neither is Chris Gregory: 'Taff was the real lifesaver,' he says. 'If he hadn't got Yvonne up, the family would have certainly died from the smoke.'

After receiving his medal for bravery, Taff has happily returned to life as normal, although he's none too happy when anyone lights a fire.

'We're very, very close,' explains Yvonne. 'After all, Taff put his own life at risk to save ours.'

Pet Casebook

Merlin the Magician

L IKE MANY YOUNG GIRLS, VICKY JONES WAS A BIG FAN OF HORSES. Encouraged by her mother Sandra, she rode and jumped a number of ponies, including her favourite, Coffee. But in 1991, when she was eight years old, she was thrown from a riding school pony and broke her back.

'I drove her across to the hospital,' remembers Sandra, 'and when I got there she was taken right away for an X-ray. We asked if they could move her to Chester Hospital, but we were told no, if we hit a bump going at two miles an hour she could be paralysed.'

It could have spelled the end of her riding career, but Vicky was not one to dismiss her own chances. When her father Graham appeared by her side on the stretcher, her first words to him were, 'I'm not giving up.'

As it happened, luck seemed to be on her side. The break was between the shoulder blades, and because it was in this location, a full recovery was possible. For the next year, Vicky undertook a painful and painstaking programme of care and physiotherapy. Finally, she was able to ride again. She had made a complete physical recovery.

But the psychological consequences of the fall were far more long-reaching. Vicky's confidence was completely shattered, and she began to have flashbacks. 'It went on for a long time,' recalls Sandra. 'It was like living with a stranger.' When she tried once more to ride Coffee, it was a disaster. 'I went on Coffee, and I just froze,' Vicky explains. 'The horse went over to my Mum, as if to say, '"get her off".' Vicky's confidence was so affected by the accident that for a while, her mother had to spend every day with her in school. 'Prior to the accident she'd been so confident she couldn't understand that you could get hurt,' explains Sandra. 'It came as a shock to her to realise that you can actually come to harm on a horse.'

As Vicky could now not even ride her own mount Coffee, her mother decided to advertise for a 'very, very safe horse'. For the next two years, Vicky and Sandra searched high and low. The first eight candidates that Vicky looked at got short shift; some she tried out for a few seconds in the saddle, and some she refused to even mount. It was looking like she would never find a suitable pony.

But horse number nine was different. As he ambled up to greet her, there was only one thing that could be said about him: he was ugly. Grey with a pink nose and black splodges, Black Beauty he wasn't. His name was Merlin, and Vicky felt instantly at home with him. Merlin was the one.

The effect was immediate. Within weeks of having Merlin, Vicky began to ride over jumps again. 'We were absolutely amazed,' remembers Sandra. 'I was almost in tears.' A new-found confidence returned to Vicky, in everything she did. Merlin and Vicky were obviously meant for one another.

Above: Vicky in pre-accident days showing an early talent for show jumping.

During their training, pony and rider built up a complete trust with one another. If, for some reason, the horse refused a jump, Vicky would never say it was Merlin's fault. If she was ready for the challenge, so was he. They soon began to enter competitions once more. And the more they entered, the more Vicky's confidence grew. Soon they were class winners at local shows and gymkhanas.

Then, in October 1995, when Vicky was twelve, they won a place at the Nationwide Unaffiliated Novice Championships. Vicky and Merlin made two clear rounds with good times. But during the jump-off, Vicky made a mistake and the one thing that everyone had been dreading happened again. She fell. But this time, although disappointed, she was unharmed. She had shown herself to be a very able jumper, and both she and Merlin had performed admirably. There was no reason to feel down-hearted.

Two weeks later, Sandra was watching Merlin take his trotting practice. But as she watched, she noticed something very peculiar. When Vicky wasn't in the saddle, Merlin would make mistakes. He would land on the poles and once he even stepped on Vicky's bike. Sandra put in a call to Steven Orrell from

the Ashbrook Equine Hospital. That evening, he arrived to put Merlin through a variety of tests. As one test passed into another, the truth dawned on everyone. It was a glaring, upsetting and deeply astonishing revelation. Merlin was blind.

But a more extraordinary twist was yet to come. Steven explained that because his cataracts were in such an advanced state, Merlin had probably been in his present state of visual impairment for at least two years.

The conclusions were startling: Merlin had been competing, very successfully, while almost totally blind. His trust in Vicky was so complete that even she did not realise that he was unable to see. He had literally heard and felt his way around the courses, guided only by Vicky's gentle commands.

But the implications of his condition were the most worrying of all. 'We were told, it's cruel to keep a blind horse,' recalls Graham. 'You can't leave it out all night, you've got to be with it when it's feeding, and so on.' Sandra and Vicky, however, were not going to be beaten that easily.

Top: Merlin won scores of rosettes and trophies before the diagnosis.

Pet File

Pet name: Merlin.

Age: 26 years.

Likes: Guinness, bacon sandwiches, carrots and fruit, and aniseed sticks; sharing mints with Vicky.

Dislikes: Breakfast and dinner being even slightly late!; silly people: once, a pub goer, instead of offering the usual ash tray of crisps, offered one of cigarette butts. But he quickly regretted it when Merlin blew the contents back all over him!

Hobbies: Making people laugh; getting kids to chase him; standing on their crisp packets; playing tug-o-war.

Right: A proud Merlin with Vicky after winning a prize at a gymkhana.

Sandra called Leahurst, Liverpool University's Large Animal Hospital. She was immediately put through to a vet called Derek Knottenbelt. His words were encouraging: 'I've done a dog, a cat, a pony, a horse and a gorilla, and the horse was the easiest.' Unfortunately, he hadn't yet seen Merlin.

'Merlin had very bad cataracts in both eyes,' explains Derek. 'I couldn't see far back into his eyes because the cataracts were so advanced. Furthermore, his pupil was not responsive, because he'd had repeated episodes of a disease we call uviatus, which is very serious and produces cataracts as a secondary effect. So that does create a considerable difference to the surgery which has to be performed.'

Far from being the easiest kind of operation to carry out, Derek Knottenbelt put Merlin's chances of surviving the highly complex operation at around three per cent, and this was an optimistic prediction. Despite the poor prognosis, both Sandra and Vicky felt they had no choice. Merlin was in terrible pain with his uviatus, and Derek was prepared to carry through the surgery, in spite of the small chances of success.

'In the vast majority of cases, a blind horse simply cannot cope with life,'

Merlin keeps up his cheeky behaviour helping himself to a quick snack.

he explains, 'and a vet will usually recommend they are put down. But I talked extensively to the people concerned and recognised that Merlin was still going to have a long, useful life. There was no doubt in my mind that Sandra and Vicky would look after the horse. Come hell or high water.'

When Merlin went into the Equine Hospital for surgery on one eye, Sandra and Vicky were quite distraught, convinced that he would have to be put down under the anaesthetic. 'The professor had told us that if the eye concerned turned to pulp in his hand he'd have no option but to give Merlin an overdose of anaesthetic,' Sandra explains. 'And destroy him.'

Mother and daughter paid Merlin a last visit, took what they knew might be

Merlin safe and sound in his stable prior to his operation.

their last photographs of him, and departed in tears. Vicky was determined everything would be all right. Sandra couldn't quite share her youthful optimism. 'I was in floods,' she admits.

The operation got underway and Derek Knottenbelt started first on Merlin's most badly-affected eye. Sandra waited by the phone, convinced it would be the worst outcome. But that same morning, to her enormous relief and joy, Derek Knottenbelt rang with the best possible news. 'It's incredible. The old trouper's sitting upright in the recovery room.'

Merlin has now gained some sight and with it a rapidly expanding fan club of devoted children. Vicky is now 13 and although she doesn't jump Merlin anymore she still rides and cares for him.

'When we heard about Merlin's blindness, she had just got her confidence back,' explains Sandra. 'I dread to think what would have happened if we'd had him put down. Two blows in three years would have been horrific. That's why we had to battle on. For both of them.' Vicky puts it more simply. 'Merlin's a fighter,' she says. 'And he always will be.'

TV Reconstruction

A Friend in Need

T HE STORY OF SASHA AND TESS ACTUALLY BEGINS WITH A DOG CALLED Sheena. Mr and Mrs Alex Roebuck had always been keen on German Shepherds. But when they saw a little ball of fur called Sheena in their local kennels, there was only one place she was going, and that was home with them.

Sheena gave the Roebucks many years of pleasure, an outgoing and loving dog with a kind nature. But when tragedy struck and she contracted diabetes, Sheena withdrew into herself. 'She'd go into a corner and wouldn't come out,' explains Alex.

Alex began wracking his brains for a way to bring her out of her torpor. As she had been a kind mother earlier in her life, he thought a new companion might be the answer. So both he and Mrs Roebuck travelled to the RSCPA kennels to find a suitable puppy.

One particular dog had only arrived that morning, a Greyhound-Collie cross called Tess. Thin, bony and awkward, she had been neglected by her previous owner and was only 12 weeks old. But the moment Mrs Roebuck picked her up, she draped her paws around her neck. 'And that was that,' says Alex. 'We'd lost the argument totally. Cheque book out.'

Alex is a confirmed dog lover, devoted to both Sasha and Tess.

Pet Files

Pet name: Sasha.

Age: 4 years.

Likes: Running; sweets and chocolate; children, especially those with sweets and chocolate.

Dislikes: Other dogs, apart from Tess.

Hobbies: Favourite plastic play train and teddybear; anything that squeaks!

Name: Tess.

Age: 7 years.

Likes: Fetching balls and sticks, especially catching them mid-air; women.

Dislikes: Most men, except Alex.

Hobbies: Chasing round in circles; stealing Sasha's dinner; occasional cups of tea (especially if Sasha's having one).

When Tess came home, she ambled nervously towards her new friend Sheena. After a brief moment of wariness, Tess and Sheena became like long lost sisters. And as the confidence grew, the dogs began to play games and playfight with each other. During these games, Sheena would always go for Tess's legs, pitching her over onto her back. Tess soon realised that this was the best way to playfight, and began to go for the front legs too. But when Sheena sadly passed on, Alex brought a new dog into Tess's life: a Siberian Husky by the name of Sasha.

'When we first got her,' recalls Alex, 'she was a gorgeous , fluffy vision. She looked like a cat, and Tess hates cats. She backed off!' But it didn't take long for Tess to realise that this 10-week-old puppy was very much a canine. From an early age, it was clear that Sasha, too, was a fan of playfighting. But her Husky instincts meant she would always go for the neck.

Little did Tess know that those instincts would one day save her life.

Playfight after playfight, Tess would launch herself at Sasha's legs, bowling her over. Winning every time. And although Sasha began to use those tactics back, she never fully shook off her instincts. Little did Tess know that those instincts would one day save her life.

Sasha grew into a loving and independent friend, who would often roam on a long lead during walks. Tess, on the other hand, preferred to stay by her master's side, although the Greyhound in her would frequently lead her off on wild goose chases. But one thing was for certain: both dogs loved their walks.

In the icy depths of February 1996, Alex, Sasha and Tess embarked on a walk that would change their lives forever. 'We'd had about ten degrees of frost,' remembers Alex, 'and pipes were bursting all over the place.' Despite the frost, that morning seemed the perfect time for a walk. The time was ten o'clock.

Alex's usual route took him and his dogs along beside the canal near his home, before looping around and heading back the same way. Following their familiar path, the two dogs adopted two common positions: Tess bounding on ahead and Sasha roaming around on the end of her thirty foot lead.

The trio walked on for 15 minutes or so, and the canal was frozen solid as far as Alex could see. Satisfied, tired and more than a little cold, he turned around and headed back for home. The dogs obediently followed suit. Walking steadily, they approached a stretch of path where the canal bank disappeared from view around a bend. In the blink of an eye, Tess dashed off around the corner and was gone.

'Tess turned the corner and I heard squawking,' Alex recalls. 'I thought "she'll be chasing those ducks again", because she often does that.' What Alex couldn't know was that at that moment Tess was only seconds away from disaster. 'I heard a crash,' he explains. 'We started running and when we got round the corner I couldn't see her anywhere.'

Alex scanned the canal. Surely she couldn't have disappeared into thin air? A number of ducks had scampered across to the other side of the ice, yet Tess was simply nowhere to be seen. But Alex's gaze was suddenly drawn to the ice on the canal, pitching and hawing with movement. And in a horrible moment of realisation, Alex knew where his dog was – she was underneath the ice.

Indulging in a playful bout of duck-chasing, Tess had ventured onto the frozen surface of the canal. But the deceptively thin ice had not been able to support her weight, and had collapsed beneath her. Struggling in the frosty waters, the ice started closing back over her head. She was trapped.

'I saw the ice moving up and down, and Tess in the middle of it,' recalls Alex, 'and I thought, "Oh my God", I knew I was going to have to wade into that canal.' Unsure how deep the canal was at this point, Alex began to look for a safe way down the bank to the edge. But as he was looking, Sasha was acting.

Every Husky has a built-in instinct for survival. In the wild, this instinct extends to hunting: when the dog spies its target, it will crouch down, stock still, tense and trembling, like a coiled spring. Then, when the time is right, it will launch itself straight at the prey. Next to Alex, Sasha was already frozen in readiness.

Alex and Sasha revisit the spot where the dramatic icy rescue took place.

'I just remember it as a grey streak,' recalls Alex, 'a mass of weight and strength crashing through the ice.' Unleashing her powerful bulk, Sasha had launched herself onto the frozen canal, shattering the surface. The force of her

The Siberian Husky

Origins: The Siberian Husky is a powerful animal developed as an all-purpose working dog by the Chukchi tribe of extreme north-eastern Siberia. Protective and loyal, the husky is an ideal family dog.

Height/weight: 53-58 cm/20 – 27 kg.

Characteristics:
- Friendly and adaptable.
- Needs a lot of exercise to avoid boredom and obesity.
- Powerful legs and shoulders with a deep chest.
- Very thick coat.
- Bred for teamwork originally, so tolerant of other dogs.

arrival was enough to free Tess's head, allowing her to get to the surface for breath.

Now Sasha was powering towards her target, preventing the ice closing around her by using her strong forelimbs as ice-breakers. From the bank Alex could only watch in amazement at the rescue attempt he was witnessing: 'Everything seemed to happen in seconds,' he recalls. 'I just couldn't believe what I was seeing.'

When Sasha reached Tess, she had only one thing in mind. She was going for the neck. Years of training from Tess had evidently gone amiss, but Sasha's instincts told her exactly what to do. Holding Tess by the scruff of the neck, the Husky was surging back to land.

As the two dogs approached, Alex was suddenly aware of the long lead, still in his hand. With valuable seconds ticking away it was the helping hand both dogs needed. Pulling with all his strength Alex hauled the heavy Husky onto the bank. Although dripping wet with icy water, Sasha waited until she was safely on dry ground before releasing her grip on Tess. 'She wasn't bothered one iota,' says Alex. 'She just shook herself off and then went to see how Tess was.'

Fearing for the shivering dog's condition, Alex wasted no time in carrying Tess home, her rescuer following close behind. After a warm bath, Tess was unsteady but comfortable, and went straight to bed, ignoring her dinner completely, which was lucky, as Sasha had worked up a considerable appetite.

Alone with a cup of tea, Alex went over the incident again and again in his mind. 'These dogs are so close together,' he explains, 'so dependent on each other because one brought the other up, and they've looked after each other. When Tess was in trouble, Sasha didn't hesitate at all.'

'I couldn't have saved her,' continues Alex. 'I'm a strong swimmer but with ten degrees of frost and iced-up water I don't know if I'd have survived. Sometimes I've thought: what would have happened if Sasha hadn't been there? Would Tess have lost her life, and me as well?'

Today, Sasha and Tess are closer friends than ever before, and Alex is confident they will stay that way. Tess is still very suspicious of water, and will only sniff around the canal bank. And Sasha? That is best left to Alex:

'She was awarded the RSPCA award for bravery. No one could be prouder of that dog than me and my wife. There's only way to describe her. She's a Wonderdog.'

Why did Sasha Save Tess?

Robert Killick, an ex-dog breeder, magazine columnist and author of many animal books, says:

'Sasha's actions may have to do with genetic memory. The Husky is used to freezing conditions. These dogs have been bred for thousands of years from the extremes of Siberia to Canada, herding reindeer and pulling sleds, and their senses are very acute.

'There's no way that anyone could prove it, but it could have been the fact that ice was involved that triggered some kind of genetic memory. Sasha would have been in her natural envirnonment: an icy one. She might have recognised Tess as a fellow pack member sending out distress signs and that might have prompted her to act.

'I hear many different stories of dogs' endeavours and I'm convinced we do not know the depths of canine sagacity. I'm not surprised Sasha jumped into the canal that day. Dogs have abilities we've barely touched on.'

Sasha receives her award from the RSPCA.

TV Reconstruction

Lady the Escapologist

'I DON'T WANT ANOTHER DOG!' TEN YEARS AGO, CHARLOTTE PALMER WENT against her better judgement and kept a little Collie pup called Lady which her son Robert had bought. She already owned a Yorkshire Terrier called Sam, and with her husband's health deteriorating, a new doggy addition to the family would mean a lot more work for her.

Even worse, this little pup turned out to be something of a tearaway. Her frequent escapes out of the garden gate or through gaps in the hedge kept Charlotte's nerves in prime condition. The roads around the village of Lulworth in Dorset (where Charlotte lives) are busy, especially in the summer, and with many farms nearby, keeping an unruly pup was more than a handful for anyone. But Charlotte decided to keep Lady. She had no way of knowing it was a decision that would one day save her life.

The summer of '95. For most people in Britain, the merry month of May was a time spent out of doors. For Charlotte, now seventy years old, the fine weather was the perfect excuse to enjoy her garden. On the fifth of May, she was passing a pleasant summer's evening sitting with Lady, her constant companion since the death of her husband eight years ago.

'It was a beautiful day,' says Charlotte, 'but it was so hot I thought I'd go in for a wee boiled egg for my tea.' She opened the

Charlotte enjoys spending time out in her garden.

door to her kitchen and walked inside. But already, she could sense there was something wrong. 'As I was coming in, I felt a tiny moment of light-headedness, nothing really. I thought it must be the heat.'

Charlotte shrugged off the feeling and began to prepare her meal. Reaching for a saucepan to boil some water, the sensation came again. 'The next thing I knew, I was on the floor,' she says.

Although she didn't know it at the time, Charlotte had experienced a minor stroke. She fell to the floor on her side, breaking her hip, and lay sprawled between the kitchen and the living room. It was an awkward fall, and she could do nothing but lie still, paralysed by pain and shock. Yet salvation was only a few feet away.

'I tried to reach the telephone,' remembers Charlotte. 'That was my lifeline. But it was just too far away. Every movement was agony.'

Charlotte made several attempts to crawl to the phone, but the pain was so excruciating that she began to slip in and out of consciousness. Time was running out and with no one expected to call for hours, time was something that Charlotte could not afford to squander. She may have lain on the floor for minutes. Perhaps hours. But when she came round again, there was a new addition to the room. It was Lady. Standing over her. Watching.

Charlotte turned and stared up at her dog's inquisitive face. Head cocked to one side, Lady was straining towards her, curious. Charlotte summoned every ounce of strength she had left: 'Get Rene ...', her voice trailed off, curtailed by a new wave of pain.

Pet file

Pet name: Lady.

Age: 10 years.

Likes: Being groomed; eating soup – all kinds, but especially Scotch Broth; playing with Charlotte's daughter's Jack Russell.

Dislikes: Nothing!

Hobbies: Running after sticks and balls in the garden; going on outings to the local cave.

Charlotte knew her neighbours Irene and Ron Kellock were probably in their garden next door. They were both devoted to Lady, and sometimes joked they almost shared her with Charlotte. Rene was a name that was familiar to Lady. Charlotte hoped she would understand.

Lady's ears twitched. Instinct told her something was wrong. She had never heard that tone in her mistress's voice before. Worried, she began pacing up and down. The command came again, louder this time. 'Go Lady, get Rene.'

As she spoke, Charlotte felt blackness descending once more. It was only a matter of time before she would lapse back into unconsciousness. She peered at Lady through hazy eyes. Even if she understood the command there was another problem: the garden was practically escape-proof. As well as being her next-door neighbours, the Kellocks had been the architects of a very special security system for Charlotte to prevent Lady's terminal wanderlust. Ron Kellock had assembled a series of tough plastic fences, hawthorn hedges and metal grilles to plug all possible gaps and escape routes.

The dog-proof garden had been built to keep Lady safe from harm. But now, the Fort Knox-style defences had turned the garden into a prison. 'I never really thought about how she could do it,' Charlotte explains, 'all I knew was that she was my last hope, my last chance.'

Not only had the Kellocks built an elaborate defence system, but Lady herself had been schooled extensively in the perils of leaving the garden. Lady was a dog who knew full well that even if a gate was open, she had to wait for

Charlotte's dog-proof garden

Charlotte's neighbour Ron Kellock, a landscape gardener, was meticulous in his planning of the ultimate escape-proof garden:

'As neighbours we're very friendly with Charlotte so we were naturally concerned when Lady kept getting out. There's a very busy road next door and that meant we had to work out a way of keeping her in for her own safety.

'If you're going to stop a dog getting out of somewhere like a garden you have to try and look at it through a dog's eyes. So I went round trying to spot the places in the hedge where you could see daylight. That done, I used various types of fencing to block them in. It took me a couple of attempts to find them all though!'

'I was surprised when Lady got out that day, especially when I realised no one had left the gate open. She's over 10 now and not as agile as she was, so it was all the more impressive. I've always

Above: Charlotte's hedge, note the wire mesh to block the gaps through to the Kellock's garden
Right: The Kellocks' garden.

thought dogs are intelligent and what Lady did was really marvellous.'

permission to leave before being allowed through. But now Charlotte was hoping against hope that Lady's instinct would override those orders. And fast.

Luckily for Charlotte, the first stage of Lady's escape was simple. Because of the hot weather, she had left the kitchen door wide open. At least Lady would have an easy route to the garden. With that thought, Charlotte sank back into unconsciousness.

Tearing into the garden, Lady wasted no time. Her first target was a hedge at the top of the garden. But Ron had done a good job. Every inch of greenery was reinforced by thick steel mesh. Lady pushed blindly against the hedge, but the harsh metal drove her back. She would have to look for another way.

Next door, the Kellocks were finishing off their garden chores and looking forward to a night out. 'We didn't hear anything out of the ordinary,' says Ron. 'No

Rough Collies

Origins: Herding dog that originated in Scotland.

Appearance: Slender but strongly-built body with broad chest and long muzzle. Heavy coat with mane.

Height/weight: 59-67 cm/22-34 kg.

Characteristics: The Collie's natural intelligence and obedience make it easy to train. Highly strung but eager to please, Collies often form a strong attachment to their owners while wary of strangers.

- Excellent watchdog.
- Loyal and affectionate.
- Well-suited to being a police or guide dog.

commotion, no fuss. Nothing to make you think there was a race against time going on next door.'

Lady looked at her options. The first hedge had been no good. The mesh had seen to that. Instead, she bounded down to the gate. It usually seemed to open if she waited long enough. But not this time. With all her options spent, there was now only one, untried, path to freedom: the hedge at the bottom of the garden. Part digging, part squeezing through the leaves and branches, Lady inched forwards. The thorns were sharp, but now raw instinct was driving her on.

Finally, through the foliage, a glimmer of light. Lady shot into the side alley adjoining the two houses. She was free at last. But as soon as one obstacle disappeared, another stood steadfastly in her way. Ron hadn't just designed his

RECONSTRUCTION

Top left: Lady sensed Charlotte's pain.

Top right: Getting out of the garden was no easy task.

Right: The Kellocks were surprised to see Lady in their garden.

neighbour's garden to keep dogs in; he had also designed his own garden to keep dogs out. In fact, the only way in to the Kellocks' property was through a harsh and prickly hawthorn hedge. Undeterred, Lady began to pull herself through.

By now, the Kellocks had almost finished in the garden. 'We were gradually working our way back to the gate,' Ron explains. 'We were just about to pack up, in fact.' But a rustling in the shrubs behind made them stop and turn. It was Lady, standing on their lawn, panting after her strenuous escape. The Kellocks were bemused as she ran up and down without barking. They could see from the hawthorns on her coat that she had come through the hedge, but she had never been round to the Kellocks' house at this time before. Unsure quite what to do, they led a reluctant Lady out and told her to go home.

Irene and Ron Kellock had known Charlotte and Lady for many years.

Shutting the gate behind them, they returned to their garden, only to find that Lady was already there, having gone through the same hedge as before. Irene explains: 'Her muzzle was damp and she had all these burrs in her fur. She'd never done anything like this before in all the years we'd known her.' In that instant, Irene knew that something was wrong.

She hurried over to Charlotte's bungalow, to find Lady already waiting for her. Entering through the open back door, she could see Charlotte's motionless body on the floor. Her friend was still breathing.

She called for her husband to come quickly, and knelt down beside Charlotte to comfort her. Charlotte's breathing quickened as she began to come round. Suddenly, her eyes flickered open, and she whispered, 'Rene? You're here!'

Little did she know the real reason for her neighbour's presence was standing close by, wagging her tail.

Doctors told Charlotte she had been in a coma while unconscious, and kept her in Poole Hospital for six weeks under observation. 'It wasn't 'til later, when Rene and Ron came to the hospital that they told me how Lady had broken through the fence and led them to me,' explains Charlotte. 'Thank goodness for good neighbours, and thank goodness for Lady.'

Pet Casebook

The Hospital Helpers

> **With Dylan, the young patients can share their fears and hopes, and confide the secrets they wouldn't dream of telling an adult.**

DYLAN IS A HOSPITAL VISITOR. ON CALL ON THE WARDS OF TWO LONDON hospitals, he brightens up the days of sick and terminally ill children. With him, the young patients can share their fears and hopes, and confide the secrets they wouldn't dream of telling an adult.

But Dylan is no ordinary visitor: off duty, he is a 2 $\frac{1}{2}$-year-old Labrador owned by Dr Hilary Summerfield. Dylan doesn't lead a regular pet's life. When other cats and dogs are spending their afternoons having a quiet kip, or waiting for their owner to take them for a walk, Dylan the Labrador is getting washed and shampooed by his owner, ready to go to work.

To the children on the wards, Dylan is more than another worker. A loving and giving dog, he replaces the cuddles and comforting touch of the children's missing parents and family pets. And in doing so, he's made many new best friends.

Dylan works his own form of animal magic through a charity called CHATA. Founded by Sandra and Ronnie Stone in 1995, the Children in Hospital and Animal Therapy Association is devoted to 'putting a smile on the face of very sick children'.

For many, the thought of a cold wet nose or a waggly tail is unorthodox therapy, to say the least. Bringing pets into hospitals is considered by some to be an unusual concept – let alone any animals that might be able to help

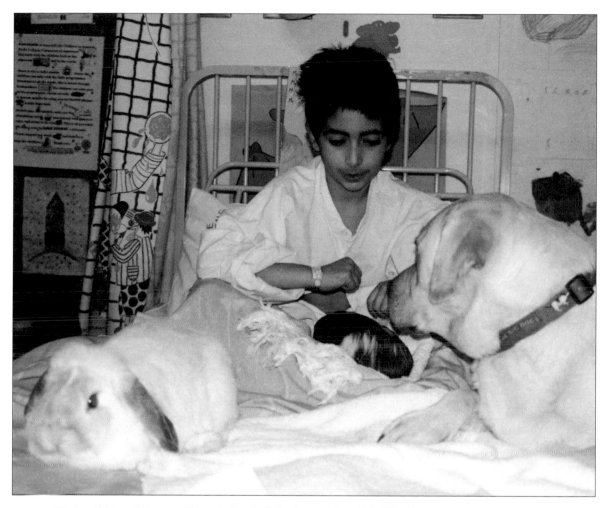

Tayfun Fehim at Queen Elizabeth Hospital, Hackney with rabbit QT, guinea-pig Squeak and Dylan.

children where human therapists have failed. But that's where Sandra's band of healthcare helpers have proved the doubters wrong.

'Just the feel of an animal can relax a fearful child who may be festooned with tubes, possibly in pain and unable to speak,' explains Sandra. 'Pets can distract children who are afraid or depressed. Psychologically it means sometimes children can give something rather than always being on the receiving end.'

CHATA is a relatively new charity, but pet therapy is not a brand new concept. Many have recognised the caring potential of pets, and Sandra has been working for some years as an animal therapist with children's hospitals and organisations, improving the quality of life of the sick or terminally ill.

Retiring as principal of a North London nursery nearly five years ago, Sandra discovered a growing interest in the relationship between children and animals. Her work with animal welfare charities was an opportunity to explore that interaction and Sandra began to take pets to visit hospices and the elderly.

For four years, Sandra and Ronnie funded the animal therapy themselves. But with an ever increasing workload and rising costs plus the need for a comprehensive scientific study on animal therapy, they needed to take matters one step further. That was when CHATA was born.

Although they are working animals, all the CHATA helpers are real pets who are dearly loved by their owners in their homes. Sandra and her husband Ronnie keep an army of animals at their home, aided by son David who is an animal warden. Their current roster reads a bit like Doctor Doolittle's walk-in surgery: six dogs, five rabbits, three guinea pigs and three chinchillas, most of which have been rescued from animal shelters.

Dillon Coker finds Dylan the dog a welcome distraction from a blood transfusion.

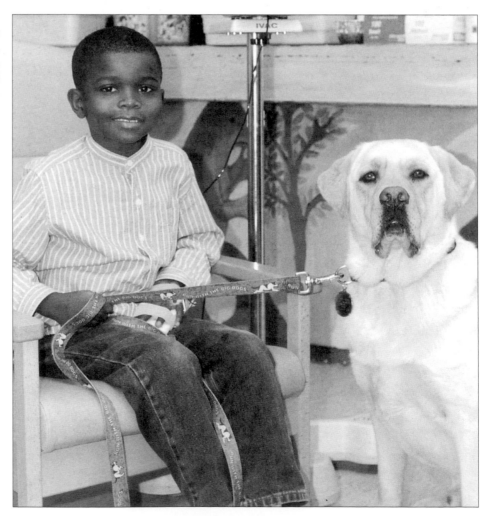

But the animals' domestic origins do not make supervision any less rigorous. CHATA pets and their human handlers are very carefully selected. Due to the delicate nature of the work, in order to qualify, both therapist and pet are required to meet highly specific criteria. Human therapists must be medical professionals or qualified with children – often as a nurse or a teacher – and they must also already keep animals in their home environment.

And it's not any pet that can qualify as an animal therapist either. Some breeds of animal are unsuitable and wouldn't be considered at all. Most are carefully chosen for their docility and warm characters. It takes a special kind of temperament to become a CHATA pet. 'Both the guinea pig and the rabbit were rescued and came in as strays to the centre where I work,' Sandra explains. 'Both are extremely patient and quiet.'

Pet temperament is one consideration, but hygiene is, of course, another. Health was a concern from the very start and an issue that CHATA addressed from the very beginning. 'At first, the main worry was cross infection and allergies,' says Sandra. 'Then it was agreed that all visiting animals should have regular veterinary checks and get certificates of zoonotic clearance.' In addition, before being allowed into each hospital, all animals are washed, and visits are approved by the infection control department at the individual hospital.

Pet file

Name of pet: Dylan.
Age: 2 $\frac{1}{2}$ years.
Likes: Going to work at the hospitals; meeting the children there; eating apples and carrots.
Dislikes: Nothing!
Hobbies: Running through the woods sniffing things; playing with other dogs; giving 'cuddles' to his family at home.

Patient John Willis loves Dylan's visits.

Great Ormond Street Children's Hospital and Queen Elizabeth Hospital, Hackney both benefit from Sandra's unique form of therapy. And it's here that Dylan makes his weekly round. 'The children look forward to Dylan coming every week,' says his owner Dr Hilary Summerfield. 'He's a wonderful dog and has the most amazing temperament. And he's crazy about the children – he always puts his heart and soul into everything. It's almost as though he realises how fragile they are.'

For the youngsters trapped in their hospital beds, watching Dylan pad into the ward to begin his visits is the highlight of the week. Some play hunt the chocolate button with him, others just want to stroke him and talk. 'It's lovely to see how much pleasure he gives them', explains Dr Summerfield. 'He's like a big teddy bear.'

And it was pleasure that Dylan gave to one child suffering from blindness and cerebral palsy. 'He wanted to go to the shops so I let him take Dylan's lead while I pushed his wheelchair down the hospital corridor,' explains Dr Summerfield. 'Then he described to us the shops he imagined we were going past. He had a tremendous imagination.'

Another Great Ormond Street resident is 12 year-old Ben Wheaton, who is in hospital for a leg operation. He finds Sandra's animals a welcome comfort after leaving his Yorkshire Terrier Annie back home in Jersey.

Above: Rose Walker gives Squeak the guinea-pig a cuddle.

Right: Jodie Duncan found Bertie the rabbit a great comfort.

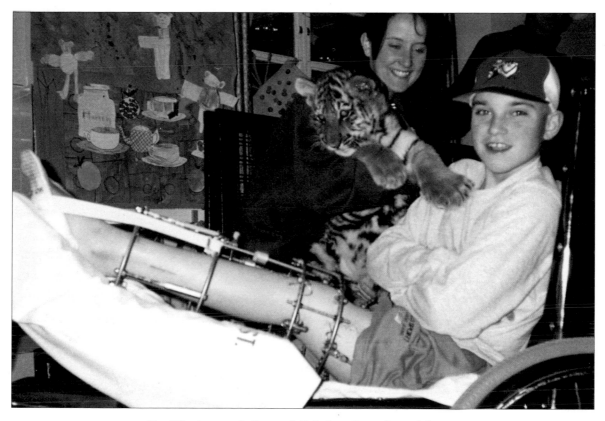

Ben Wheaton meets tiger cub Kalush at Great Ormond Street.

His mother Jackie remembers being shocked at first to see rabbits, a Labrador and a guinea-pig on the ward. 'But then I saw how Ben's eyes and those of all the children light up. The animals relieve the tension of some of these horrendous operations.'

For 10 year-old Jodie Duncan, life had taken a turn for the worse. She had lost her hair and developed ugly lesions all over her body after lengthy chemotherapy for a disease of the immune system. As depression sunk in, she showed no interest in anything and refused to communicate with anybody.

Then she told a doctor how much she missed her dog. Staff contacted CHATA and asked for help. Next time Sandra went into the hospital she brought a very special companion: Bertie, a big white and brown rabbit. But Jodie scowled as the rabbit was put in her lap, so Sandra left Bertie and retreated.

'After a while Jodie began to tell Bertie all of her troubles,' Sandra explains. 'The rabbit was the key to unlocking her depression. She was able to talk about her anxiety and she became a lot happier.'

THE CHATA MOTTO
Animals are an emotional barometer. When you're feeling down and cloudy they bring in the sunshine and brighten up your life.

After a year in hospital, Jodie, now 13, is back at school and busy looking after her pet fish in their aquarium, her lizards and her West Highland Terrier, Josh. To her mother Janis the change is undeniable. 'It has been amazing,' she says. 'I've absolutely no doubt that the animal visits helped greatly. They were the only thing that gave her any interest.'

And Jodie isn't the only child that has benefitted from the attention of Sandra's band of Florence Nightingale pets. The cases are numerous.

Sandra recalls the story of a little girl who had been at Great Ormond Street for four years and loved a particular rabbit. The rabbit visited her up until the girl died. It attended her memorial service and the parents arranged for the headstone on her grave to take the form of a rabbit, a testimony to the significance they felt the pet had held in their daughter's short life.

Then there is the blind, autistic child who was living in a virtual vacuum. One day, Sandra passed when he was lying listless on the floor. She put the rabbit to his head and suddenly his arm came up and he stroked the pet. 'The experience really calmed him down,' Sandra explains.

Many children are longing to be able to 'give' something again.

After years of research, Sandra is still discovering more and more about the special links that are possible between pets and children. She's realised that after lengthy periods in hospital suffering pain and horrendous treatments, many children are longing to be able to 'give' something again. Nurturing, feeding, and cuddling the animals provides a perfect outlet, allowing the child to take responsibility and to be the carer rather than to be cared for.

As the charity takes off, Sandra aims to set up a local supporters' group to raise funds. Then there's a regular newsletter to get off the ground as well. In addition, she aims to organise programmes involving therapeutic horse riding, taking a donkey into play centres in hospitals and eventually offering very sick children a chance to swim with wild dolphins.

For the moment, though, the weekly work of pets like Dylan and Bertie goes on, providing a valuable link for sick children to the outside world. Sandra knows that to a child trapped in a hostile environment of white corridors, drips and needles, a homely dog like Dylan wagging his tail or a fluffy bunny like Bertie wrinkling his nose can change everything.

As Jodie's mother Janis says: 'If I hadn't seen it myself, I would never have believed the difference animals can make. It's miraculous.'

Pet Casebook

Chrissie the Lifesaver

JOAN AND WALTER BERRY LIVE IN BANGOR, COUNTY DOWN, ALONG WITH their eight dogs and four cats. The couple share a deep love of animals and used to run a boarding kennels. Although they now only have their own eight dogs left, they use one of the kennel blocks to help house them. 'They're always let out and have the run of the house as well,' explains Joan. 'But it gives us all more space.'

Joan is a Champion show judge, and certainly knows her dogs. Chrissie, their German Shepherd came from first-class breeding stock. 'Even though we got her age two, she blended into the family as a unit and just wanted to be part of everything,' Joan explains. 'She has a wonderful temperament.'

From the start, Chrissie built up a strong rapport with Walter. 'They've always had this special bond,' Joan explains. 'Chrissie's always on the alert and very watchful of people and she spends ages just watching and waiting for Walter.' It was this special relationship between dog and master that came into play one summer morning in August in a dramatic way that no one could have expected, or predicted.

Chrissie and Joan have a very close relationship.

The German Shepherd Dog

Origins: Originally used for herding, guarding and farming duties, this large, powerful dog makes an excellent house and guard dog. Its high training potential makes it ideal for obedience work. A loyal dog, the German Shepherd can become highly attached to and protective of its master and his property.

Height/weight: average 63 cm/average 31 kg.

Characteristics:

- Multi-talented working dog favoured as a police and army dog for its loyalty, intelligence and protective instincts.
- Needs knowledgeable handling from puppyhood.
- High intelligence makes for ease of training.
- Has an excellent nose which makes it ideal for tracking and rescue work.

Joan is a champion show judge whose dogs have won many prizes over the years.

The time was 7 am. Walter had risen early along with Joan. 'He was so bright and breezy that I got up too,' she remembers. 'I thought, better get going, no lying in bed if he's up!' The couple ate breakfast together in the kitchen and then while Joan went up to the kennels to look after the dogs, Walter returned outside. He was in the middle of a big job – converting a recently purchased Land Rover from petrol to diesel with the help of his son.

'I've been an engineer all my life,' Walter explains. ' First as a motor mechanic and then I had a garage of my own. Plus my father before me was in the motor trade so I've been associated with it since I was a boy.'

This particular morning, Walter had decided to make an early start by himself. After all, it was a straightforward procedure. He'd designed a part for the chassis and was keen to tack it on and check the mechanics. But his eagerness was soon to prove a costly mistake.

Working at the front of the house, he quickly extracted the engine out of the car. Engrossed in his work, Walter was keeping an eagle eye out for the practicalities of the job, but in doing so he failed to notice one small detail: the petrol that was slowly dripping onto his overalls.

'The petrol pipe from the engine had been put to the back,' explains Walter. 'That should have been safe enough, but what I didn't know was that it had fallen down, below the level of the fuel tank, which was pretty much full. Petrol had got over my overalls and the floor ... '

Over the other side of the yard, and well out of hearing distance, Joan was attending to the dogs' breakfast in the kennels. It was the usual scene of running water, barks and wagging tails. 'It's very difficult to hear anything with all the noise going on,' Joan explains.

The dogs eagerly ate their morning snacks. All except one. Far from behaving normally, Chrissie the German Shepherd was jumping up and down at the door, higher and higher. 'It was like the wall of death if you've ever seen

Pet File

Name: Chrissie.

Age: 6 years.

Likes: Life and people, especially children, eating Bonios; wagging her tail; giving sloppy kisses to horses!

Dislikes: Not much.

Hobbies: Bumping into things; running along the beach throwing bits of seaweed in the air; chasing seagulls and failing to catch them!

it,' remembers Joan. 'She was just throwing herself at the door leaping about eight feet off the ground.'

The other three dogs were nonplussed, as was Joan. There seemed no explanation at all for Chrissie's strange behaviour. 'I kept saying: "Now Chrissie will you stop that",' recalls Joan, 'and I was thinking: " What's going on?"' But far from obeying her mistress, Chrissie started to make even more noise. 'She suddenly made this horrific sound,' says Joan. 'It wasn't a bark or a howl. I don't know how to describe it. It was a strange animal noise. But every hair on my body stood up.'

At that moment Joan knew something was badly wrong. 'Chrissie was jumping at the door like a Jack in the Box,' Joan explains. ' And it was then that I heard Walter shouting my name.' Joan let the dog out of her kennel. When the door opened, Chrissie shot into the yard, flying across the ground faster than Joan had ever seen her run before. Joan followed. And what she saw stopped her in her tracks.

Staggering towards her was a terrible vision. A man engulfed in blue flames, silently holding his hand up like a piece of black driftwood. It was Walter. The welding torch he had lit only moments previously had sparked the petrol on his clothes. Seconds later, Walter had become a ball of flames.

'The whole thing went up in seconds,' Walter remembers. 'It was a real struggle for me to get out from the chassis because I was on fire.' Rolling himself up in a piece of carpet, he'd tried to extinguish the fire but it was useless. 'The material turned out to be full of petrol and oil and only made matters worse,' Walter recalls. 'I really thought I'd had it then.' In agony, he had dragged himself through two garages and into the yard, desperate for help.

'The sight was so traumatic I'll never forget it as long as I live,' Joan recalls. 'The flames were 10 or 12 feet high, and smoke was coming off his hands. I felt I was watching my husband burning to death before my eyes.'

In seconds, Joan reached for a hose. She trained the water on Walter until the flames

Walter is still recovering from his injuries.

went out. 'He just stood there, not saying anything,' she remembers. 'It was awful.'

Meanwhile, Chrissie was keeping out of the way. 'She's the type of dog that is very affectionate and always wants to get up as close as possible to you,' explains Joan. 'But as she ran up to Walter, she just put the brakes on, sat down and never said a thing. She just watched me hose him down.'

Joan took Walter into the kitchen, with Chrissie in tow. Walter's clothes had been burnt off by the flames, and now he was naked apart form the scraps of overall that still clung to his left leg and to his boots. 'I cut the rest of his clothes off,' Joan remembers. 'And all the time Chrissie was just looking up at me with these huge liquid brown eyes as if to say what are we going to do?'

Joan drove Walter, 'like Damon Hill', to the nearest hospital where doctors arranged an ambulance to rush him to the Burns Unit at The Royal Victoria Hospital. Back home she found Chrissie waiting anxiously.

'I found all these little fires had started when I got back,' Joan explains. 'It was all the bits of clothing that had dropped off Walter as he ran to the yard. There was literally a trail of small flickering flames.'

Extinguishing the fires, Joan reassured the German Shepherd. 'Chrissie just clung to me,' Joan remembers. 'She put her paws around my neck and practically gave me a hug. It was then I knew that she was not only a remarkable animal but an animal who'd saved my husband's life.'

Walter is now out of hospital but still has to sleep on a water or sand bed to help with his injuries. Neither he nor Joan are in any doubt about the actions of their German Shepherd:

'We have one dog that's fully trained,' Walter explains. 'Now if that dog had been the one to act it wouldn't have surprised me so much. But Chrissie is different. I think she came to my aid because she's fond of me and knew I was in trouble. She's a very special dog.'

Joan agrees. 'It was as if she sensed Walter's need before hearing his cry of help', she explains. 'Without Chrissie, Walter would have died. There's no doubt about it.'

> **Chrissie was just looking up at me with these huge liquid brown eyes as if to say what are we going to do?**

HIGH JUMP HISTORY
Stag, an 18 month-old Lurcher leapt into the record books with a 3.8 m (12$\frac{1}{2}$ ft) jump over a smooth wooden wall at the annual Cotswold County Fair, Cirencester, in 1993. It was the highest canine high jump ever recorded.

TV Reconstruction

Beauty to the Rescue

WINIFRED SKIFF IS A VERY DEDICATED LADY WHO ADORES ANIMALS. Although nearly 75, she devotes herself to running the Silverlake Sanctuary in Hampshire. It's a special establishment catering for a specific type of guest as Winn explains: 'It's the only animal sanctuary I know of that's for elderly animals. They're like me – old!'

Winn founded and built the sanctuary from scratch 36 years ago, spending her own money on renovating caravans, re-roofing hutches, and anything else that would give the animals comfortable roofs over their head. Now Silverlake is home to a burgeoning family of assorted animals. The full cast list runs as follows: 89 cats, 4 dogs, 2 horses, 1 donkey, 2 sheep, 4 goats, 10 rabbits, 2 geese, 4 chickens, 2 guinea pigs, and 2 ducks. All rub shoulders together happily and without the slightest disagreement.

That peace and harmony should find a place at Silverlake is hardly surprising. Winn has been collecting and caring for animals since she was a young teenager. 'It was sixty years ago, when I was 15, that I found a cat abandoned in an alleyway,' she remembers. 'Then gradually I built up a collection of animals until my mother said I could carry on my ballroom dancing hobby or give it up and look after them. Of course I chose the animals. I just couldn't abandon them.'

Other workers at the sanctuary have also witnessed Winn's caring ways first-hand: 'Animals always come tops in her eyes,' explains Eileen Mann, a

Pet File

Name: Beauty.

Age: 26 years.

Likes: Apples, carrots and dog biscuits; being groomed.

Dislikes: Sweet biscuits.

Hobbies: Spending time with special friend Trudy the donkey; nudging people's backsides for fun when they're not looking!

volunteer worker. 'I've never met anyone to equal her in that respect. She's unique – a one-woman band.'

But with well over 100 full-time residents, running the animal sanctuary is also an exhausting job. The punishing schedule demands a daily 6 o' clock start in order to feed the animals, clean their hutches, caravans, and stables, and muck out. Not the kind of work that many 75 year-olds willingly put themselves through, especially not ones who have been in and out of hospital and suffer from a painful condition like osteoporosis – a weakening of the bones and joints.

'Winn might be slowing down a little bit but she still soldiers on,' Eileen explains. 'Her energy is incredible. And she's a very strong character, very determined.'

Winn has needed to call on that same determination in both her professional and personal life. As an animal mentor she's witnessed appalling cases of cruelty and suffering. Two of the victims are still at the sanctuary. There's Benny – the oversized goat who was brought up on the bottle after being abandoned, and then there's Beauty.

Left to graze in a forest by her elderly owners, Beauty the pony was blind in one eye when Winn rescued her. 'She was so well behaved and she didn't have any vices,' Winn explains. 'I couldn't see her put down.' But despite the

Winn has built up the thriving Silverlake Sanctuary especially for elderly animal residents.

rescue, Beauty's vision continued to deteriorate. Winn could only watch in despair as the virus that was causing Beauty's blindness took a firm grip. Eventually, the brave pony was condemned to a life of darkness. It seemed a cruel twist of fate.

Ironically enough, at the same time, Winn realised her own sight was failing. She, too, suffered the total loss of sight in one eye, with the other struggling to compensate. 'An affinity sprang up between us,' she explains. 'I know how frustrating it is not to have good sight so I began to teach Beauty commands.'

The old pony proved a remarkably quick learner. Soon she had mastered the art of stopping and starting and could sense when Winn was comforting and praising her. 'I always used to reassure her that everything's all right,' Winn explains. 'And I'd often just tell her: "Don't you worry Beauty. Nobody's going to hurt you", again and again.' As for scolding – there was rarely any need. Beauty was the epitome of obedience.

With the passing years, pony and mistress developed a level of communication that was both deep-seated and rare. And it was this ability that would come into play one extraordinary day when events at the sanctuary took an unforseen and unfortunate turn for the worse.

It was a cold, harsh late afternoon in February. Rain lashed the roofs and rattled the latches of the sanctuary. Outside, as night began to fall, Winn laboured to feed the horses. 'It was such a horrible day that they'd been in their stables quite a lot,' she recalls. ' So although I normally just muck them out in the mornings I thought I should do it again.'

Winn set about her task with her last ounces of energy, dragging the heavy bags behind her, out across the nearby field. As she did so, the rain beat down relentlessly, soaking Winn, her clothes, and the already sodden ground beneath her. It was at that point that disaster struck. 'I put my foot down and tried to pull it out of the ground but I lost my boot,' she explains. 'Then I slipped and fell backwards ... '

It was exactly the kind of fall that aggravated Winn's medical condition and the resulting pain was excruciating. Lying on her back, Winn was as good as stuck until someone came to help. But by now all the Silverlake helpers had gone home. As for passers-by – in the high winds and sleet-driven rain, help was unlikely to be close at hand.

It was then that Winn noticed a creeping sensation inching up her body. Trousers, anorak, hair ... it was reaching up as far as her shoulders. Suddenly, she

RECONSTRUCTION

Beauty set out to find her mistress.

realised that the cold mass weighing her down was mud. Winn was lying in a field that was fast turning into a massive bog. And she was slowly sinking. 'It was then that I panicked,' Winn recalls. 'I was very afraid and it felt quite spooky. Then I started to cry, but there wasn't much point because no one could hear me. I remember calling out: "What am I going to do?"'

In the stables, the horses were making the best of the terrible weather and settling down for the night. All except one. Beauty couldn't rest easy. Something was wrong and Winn's desperate voice on the wind only confirmed it. Guiding herself by instinct alone, the blind pony inched out of the stables, stumbling as she did. Then, pricking up her ears for guidance, she came to Winn's rescue.

'I looked and through the darkness I saw this huge shape,' remembers Winn. 'I thought – oh no, it's Beauty and she's not going to see me and trample all over me. So I screwed myself up and yelled: "Whoa Beauty, whoa there!"'

The blind pony stopped instantly, grateful for the direction from her mistress. A few moments passed, and Beauty began to orientate herself to Winn's voice once more. 'She was advancing, backing on to me,' remembers Winn. 'She knew I was around somewhere, and it was as if she was trying to sense where I was. She stopped about six inches away.' Lying in the mud, looking up at Beauty's tail, Winn suddenly had a thought. The arthritis in her arms was agonising, but with her remaining strength Winn lifted up her arm and reached up towards the slowly swishing tail. 'My hands were so cold I was crying,' remembers Winn, 'But I reached up and grabbed her tail. And I said, "Beauty, walk on. Walk on Beauty."'

Very slowly, Beauty began to move. Struggling to retain her grip on the tail, Winn concentrated on giving Beauty some encouragement. 'When she started to move forward, I said, "Go on Beauty, good girl."'

RECONSTRUCTION

She found Winn helpless in the mud.

Tubbs, Trudy and Beauty are all great friends.

It was beginning to work. The mud squelched behind Winn's head, and a few yards later she could feel it relinquish its hold on her. She was on firmer ground. Rolling over onto her side, Winn struggled to her feet against the onslaught of rain and wind. 'I bent double going into the stables,' she recalls, 'then I collapsed on a bail of straw. I just sat there for a while, shaking, and crying. I was in a hell of a state.'

After a warm bath and a dry set of clothes, Winn set off for the stables once more, this time with a large bag of chocolate drops, determined to make a proper fuss of her special horse. She knew full well that if it hadn't been for Beauty, hypothermia would soon have set in. Beauty had almost certainly saved her life.

'I think I was rescued to do more animal work,' explains Winn with her great generosity of spirit. 'That's how I look at it. I will never forget what Beauty did, until the day I die.'

ON THE HOOF

Toy horse Countess Natushka is the smallest full-grown horse in the world standing at only 69 cm (27 in) tall.

Pet Casebook

The Case of the Missing Cockatoo

T HERE ARE NOT THAT MANY COCKATOOS IN BRITAIN WHO ARE QUITE LIKE Primrose. Of course, there are undoubtedly birds in the land who have chosen the winning numbers on the National Lottery; there are surely birds who have flown hundreds of miles to find their owners; and there are certainly birds who have been stolen and then recovered. But Primrose is different.

Primrose is a sulphur-crested cockatoo. A cockatoo who foiled the burglar who was trying to steal him. 'Primrose is one of a kind,' says Gerry Gilbert, a bird expert in West London. 'Every so often you will get a bird that is exceptional, but not very often.'

Primrose belongs to Ms Sacha Hinds, who manages Pets Are Us, a pet shop in Ealing, West London. She is devoted to her cockatoo, and tries to spend as much time with him as possible. 'I take him in the car whenever I can,' she explains. 'I take him shopping, he just sits on my shoulder. And he sleeps in my bed sometimes. He loves

Sacha and Primrose have an affectionate relationship.

it.' Gerry Gilbert, whose own aviary contains tens of exotic birds, has known Sacha for several years, ever since Sacha came to him to buy a few birds for her shop. 'When she went on holiday, she would ask if I could look after Primrose for her,' he remembers. 'She would call up at 11.30 at night, from the airport, and want to come here to pick him up before she even went home. That bird's her life.'

It's easy to see why Primrose had such an effect on Sacha. As well as being a very handsome bird, he is immensely affectionate, not to mention talented. 'As soon as he hears my car pull up,' says Sacha, 'he calls out, "Sacha, Sacha, what are you doing?"' Primrose is also an accomplished dancer, preferring a bench to a nightclub, and Aretha Franklin to Oasis. 'He loves my soul tapes,' continues Sacha, 'It's more of a beat thing.'

Needless to say, Primrose's personality has made him many friends along the street where he lives. Every shopkeeper knows and loves him, and he in turn will like nothing better than to pass the time of day with any old ladies or children that happen to pass by. His friendliness is unprecedented. 'He really is unusual,' explains Gerry

Pet File

Name: Primrose
Age: 5 years.
Likes: Going shopping with Sacha; soul music; dancing.
Dislikes: No one (unfortunately).
Hobbies: Chewing things; being friendly to Ealing residents.

Gilbert. 'Yes, lots of birds are friendly, but with their owner, not with a complete stranger.'

Primrose's outgoing character also made teaching him to talk a pleasure. 'When I got him in 1994, all he said was, "hello",' Sacha says. 'Now he says lots of things. He mimics dogs barking, doors creaking, and says things like "Hello beautiful."' The process of teaching Primrose tricks was also a matter of building trust. The more times Sacha took him from home, the more Primrose wanted to go out. Soon the two of them were inseparable companions.

Until one day, when Primrose's friendliness became his downfall.

'It was Friday 3rd November', remembers Sacha. 'I wasn't in the shop, I was having a day off. One of the girls was on duty.' As usual, Primrose was occupying his perch near the door, squawking a greeting to his favourite customers. 'The assistant was on her own, distracted with another customer,' continues Sacha. 'So she didn't see what this guy was doing.'

Primrose charms everyone he meets.

It just took a second. But it was only when Sacha returned to the shop that she noticed the terrible truth. Primrose was gone. 'I went mad,' recalls Sacha. 'I went hysterical. I phoned the police several times and said, "this isn't just some budgie that's flown out of the window."' It was no slur on budgies, but the cry of someone whose loved one was gone. 'That day I phoned every pet shop in London, every RSPCA, bird aviary, every person I could think of,' continues Sacha. 'I also asked pet shop owners if they'd had any new customers in buying parrot stuff.'

But the calls were in vain. It was difficult to miss a bird like Primrose, but no cockatoo matching his description was to be found in London. He had simply disappeared without a trace. Being a trusting bird, Primrose had no doubt hopped happily on to his captor's shoulder, little realising he was walking out of Sacha's life. 'For a bird like Primrose, you'd probably be asking £1,000 or more,' explains Gerry Gilbert. 'And he's a cock bird. Normally cock birds only go to hens, and vice versa. But Primrose is happy to be handled by both men and women, which is why the man was able to steal him so easily.'

The close network of Primrose fans in Ealing were mobilised into action. Everyone was on the lookout, from the men in the furniture shop to the old ladies in the hairdressers. The local paper ran a front-page story. Notices appeared throughout the area: 'Primrose Has Gone.' There was nothing that Sacha would not do to get her bird back. 'I was calling up local radio stations,' she remembers. 'I called up chat shows, even if what they were talking about had nothing to do with cockatoos!'

The vigilance continued, until one day, when a man fitting the thief's description came back into Sacha's shop. 'I wasn't certain it was him, as none of the staff who saw the guy were working that day,' Sacha recalls. 'I couldn't just call the police and ask them to come down and arrest him.'

The man asked Sacha about prices of birds, and left promptly afterwards. Sacha watched him leave, and enter the off-licence down the road. 'When he came out, he saw the woman from the hairdresser's standing on the corner. I was standing outside my shop, and he obviously thought, "I've been rumbled."'

He sprinted down the road. Sacha gave chase, but he was too quick for her. Leaping into a car, he sped away – but not before Sacha had a good look. 'I got part of the car registration,' she explains, 'but now I was frightened. He might panic, and try to get rid of the bird.'

The search for Primrose stepped up a gear. Sacha called the police, with a description of the man, and the car registration as she remembered it. PC Steve Selly was dealing with the case: 'When I first spoke to Sacha, she was distraught,' he remembers. 'It was like it was her kid.' The police had classed Primrose as shoplifted goods, and the description that Sacha had given seemed to fit another suspect

Primrose loves going out shopping with Sacha.

they already had under surveillance for other crimes. The next morning, the police did a bust on a flat in Dollis Hill.

'We went in, and there was a bird in a cage in the corner that was far too small for it,' remembers PC Selly. 'It was filthy and depressed-looking. But our man was saying it was his, and he'd been given it by his sister. And he said its name was Billy. We took the bird up to the squad office. We obviously couldn't put him in a plastic bag with a label on it like most stolen goods.'

For Sacha, the call did not come soon enough. 'They told me they'd asked the guy why he had the bird in the cage,' she recalls. 'And he said because it chews things. I thought, "That's Primrose alright!"' She was out of the house in minutes.

A bundle of nerves and trepidation, Sacha went down to the police station to identify her bird. If this really was Primrose, she knew that he had a tiny microchip implanted on his skin for this very purpose. Identifying him would be a matter of routine, and the two of them could go home that afternoon.

> **'As soon as Sacha walked into the office, she said, "that's my bird".'**

'As soon as Sacha walked into the office, she said, "that's my bird",' remembers PC Selly. 'She opened the cage and the bird walked straight up her shoulder, nuzzled her, and didn't move. It stayed there. She was ecstatic.' But unfortunately, the police needed some solid proof.

Sacha, Primrose and PC Selly paid a visit to the vet to check on the bird's microchip. Sacha knew it was only a matter of minutes before Primrose could come home. But that was when disaster struck. 'The microchip had gone,' remembers Sacha. 'I was in despair.'

Occasionally birds can peck out their microchips, which are no bigger than a grain of rice. But for Sacha this was now a major problem. The police needed solid evidence that this was definitely Primrose.

Sacha took Primrose and PC Selly down to Ealing. Back on his home turf, Primrose quickly got back into the swing of things, and up to his old tricks. 'Sacha described what Primrose would do before he did it,' remembers PC Selly. 'Within a couple of minutes there's a flock of old ladies around him, and he's running up and down the bench, puffing up his crest, whistling and shouting. But we still needed more evidence, and some sort of statement from Sacha.'

It was WPC Isobel Scott who took Sacha, and Primrose, into the interview room. 'I needed it on record that she thought this particular bird was

Primrose is a local star.

definitely hers,' she explains. 'It was a straightforward interview, except that she had a bird sitting on her shoulder.'

Sacha was too worried for words. 'I had this terrible feeling that I just wasn't going to be able to prove he was mine,' she remembers, 'and the toe-rag who'd stolen him was going to be able to keep him.' Luckily for Sacha, she didn't have to say a word. Her cockatoo spoke on her behalf. He said: 'Hello, my name's Primrose'. 'All of a sudden, the bird makes a statement,' recalls WPC Scott. 'So I wrote it down.'

Primrose had taken his case into his own hands, but the suspect still insisted the bird was his. In the trial that followed, a judge found the man guilty of handling stolen goods, and sentenced him to 15 months in prison.

'When we got back I put him on the bench, and he did a little dance,' recalls Sacha. 'He was so happy to be back.'

TV Reconstruction

Blake's Incredible Journey

Tony Balderstone is a Norfolk sheep farmer. He works long, hard hours, and like many in his trade a large proportion of his daily routine revolves around three very talented dogs, each with their own unique personality. The wisest of the three was a ten-year-old collie called Blake.

Many people who spend a great deal of time with their animals talk of special bonds that grow between them, an understanding that goes beyond the norm. Tony's experience with his working dogs is just the same. Each year in September, Tony moves his sheep from Letheringsett South to Little Fransham, where they remain until January. He transports his flock by road, and this means a gruelling series of five two-hour round trips in the truck. For the ten hours that he is away, he will leave the remainder of his sheep under the care of Blake. 'I really know my dogs,' explains Tony. 'And over the last ten years I've spent more time with him than anybody.'

In August 1995, Tony was working with Mirk, one of his canine trio on the Cley Nature Reserve, near Holt, where some of his sheep had strayed onto grazing land for cattle. Meanwhile, Blake and Roy, his other two dogs, were waiting patiently in Tony's Land Rover and trailer for their master to return.

Pet File

Name: Blake.

Age: 11 years.

Likes: Working' especially taking sheep across streams and rivers; having a rest in Tony's Land Rover.

Dislikes: Too much other doggie company – likes time on his own.

Hobbies: Pushing his nose into Tony's hands in the morning; having a run around with the other dogs.

Tony and Blake have a special bond.

But when his work was done, Tony returned to find a terrible surprise was in store. 'When I got back to where the Land Rover should have been, it was gone,' he remembers, 'with Roy and Blake in the back.'

Immediately, he contacted his old friend Bernard Bishop, a warden at the reserve, and they informed the police of the theft. Bernard then suggested that they ring Radio Norfolk, who understood how important Tony's dogs were to his livelihood, and broadcast the registration number of the vehicle. 'Tony was so worried,' remembers Bernard, 'he was running around all over the place, very distressed. He was more concerned about the fact that his dogs were in the back. They're part of his life, they're with him all day.' Tony was committed to getting the two dogs back. 'I was heartbroken,' he explains. 'I spend 17 hours a day with those dogs and I trained them myself.'

As well as calling the police, another highly effective search team was mobilised: the Norfolk network of tractor drivers, game-keepers, farmers and other locals who know both Tony and his dogs. 'If Tony could do it, he'd do anything for you,' explains Bernard. 'That's why he had so many offers of help. They knew that if the shoe was on the other foot, Tony would be the first person to ring up to say, "What can I do to help?"'

The search began at 1 pm on Wednesday. Tony set about chasing a myriad of sightings in a 50 mile radius around his home, using another Land Rover which he had been offered by Kim and Robin Coombes, who own the land at Bayfield Hall, Letheringsett. It was to be a long and emotionally shattering series of journeys.

Tony was committed to getting the two dogs back.

The first sighting of Blake occurred early the next morning, around 6.45. Nick, Tony's son, is a civil engineer and was working on a site about 200 metres from the A47 at Swaffham. 'I glanced around and saw a Collie dog and could instantly tell it was Blake by his stance,' he explains. 'I tried to call him but he wouldn't obey, although he did turn round and acknowledge me.' Nick ran out to the road, calling and calling for Blake, until finally jumping into his car to pursue him, but by that stage it was too late. 'I saw him going across a field,' continues Nick. 'I turned to follow him up a farm track, but when I got up there he veered off and ran into the woods, where I lost him.' Nick called his father at 7 am, who was relieved to hear that Blake was alive and well.

Nick was the first of some twenty people who would see Blake over the next six days. But not everyone who saw him was aware of who he was. Mrs Mallen helps her husband to run their farm near Little Fransham, five miles east of Swaffham. She was driving along the A47 when she saw a Border Collie walking along the side of the road. 'It was looking very bedraggled,' she recalls. 'I did wonder who it might belong to, but it looked like it really knew where it was going.'

That night, a call came in to the Balderstones from Tony's cousin, a policeman at Swaffham. Roy had been found, taken in by a woman in Downham Market after she discovered him in her garden. She had taken him to the kennels in Wisbech. Being a young and sociable dog, it was no surprise to Tony that he was the first to be found. But Blake posed a wholly different problem. 'He's a quieter dog than Roy,' explains Tony. 'He won't approach anyone but me.'

Knowing that Blake is a good working dog, Tony wondered if, instead of heading north from Swaffham to Fakenham, Blake might go on to Little Fransham, where he pastures the sheep in the winter on the Mallens' land. Calling Mrs Mallen on the Friday morning, she confirmed that she had indeed seen a Border Collie, which she and her husband now realised had been Blake.

When sightings of Blake started moving north over the next day and a half, Tony knew that his dog was heading for home. One of the sightings came from Don Cedric, the gamekeeper at Melton Constable. He had recognised

Above: Bernard Bishop, warden at the Cley Nature Reserve.

Above right: Tony's son Nick spotted Blake as well.

Right: Blake's incredible journey.

Blake on Sunday morning, at the side of a field beside Melton Hall. He managed to get within fifty or sixty metres of Blake and shut him into a deer enclosure, a 15 acre segment surrounded by a high fence. The lowest point was a 2 metre wall. Surely now Blake was going to stay put. He picked up the phone and called Tony.

But when Tony excitedly arrived, Blake was gone, the high wall proving no obstacle at all. 'He was on the move,' explains Don. 'And when they're on the move there's no holding them.' The search kicked back into action. Perhaps Blake was heading home after all, and would stop there.

Sure enough, on Sunday at lunch time there came a call from Kim Coombe, saying that Blake was in their yard at Bayfield Hall, only 1½ miles from home. When Tony arrived, Blake was already lying low, corralling the sheep. He was thin, bedraggled, and limping with sore paws. But he was home, and still managed to wag his tail, overjoyed to see his master.

'He looked at me for a few seconds,' remembers Tony, 'and I believe he was wondering if he was going to get in trouble for being late. But then he just came up to me, put his head against me, and that was that.'

It was only a matter of days before Blake had rested up and was back to work. 'I tried to keep him inside, but he thought he was being punished,' says Tony. 'So I just let him out and he was happy again.'

Kim Coombe alerted Tony when Blake arrived at Bayfield Hall (right).

Tony with his dogs Roy (left) and Blake (right).

Tony isn't that surprised at Blake's incredible journey that spanned 50 miles. 'If you knew the dog, then you'd understand,' he says. 'I always knew he would make it back home.' But other friends remain amazed. 'It was wonderful he found his way back,' says Bernard Bishop. 'We just don't know how bright dogs are.'

Tony's wife Enid is also full of praise. 'Blake is devoted to my husband,' she says. 'Getting home was a fantastic achievement and we are very proud of him.'

Pet Casebook

Jasmine, the Cat who Cared

Audrey Fisher had always wanted a cat, and now she had qualified as a nurse and had a place of her own, there was one kind of cat in particular she had her eye on. 'My mum had a Persian Blue called Brodie,' explains Audrey, 'and she gave me the number of the place where she got him. I called up and went to see Jasmine, who was Brodie's little sister. She was one week old, and I counted the days until I could take her home.'

Jasmine quickly settled in at Audrey's new house, a small sandstone cottage in Oxton, Birkenhead, and it soon became clear that there was only one person in Jasmine's life: Audrey. 'She's always been very much my daughter's cat,' agrees Audrey's mother Marion. 'When she picks her up, Jasmine makes the usual kind of purr. But if anyone else picks her up, she makes a strange noise. It's not so much a growl as a "don't pick me up" ... she's a one-woman cat, no question.'

Audrey's exhausting routine working in a nursing home meant that she wasn't always able to see Jasmine as much as she would have liked. But whenever she got home from a long shift, she could always be sure that Jasmine would be there to welcome her back in her customary way: 'What usually

Pet File

Name: Jasmine.

Age: 10 months.

Breed: Persian Blue.

Likes: Pizza (especially ham and pineapple); Chinese food; cornflakes; bread; any beer; being driven around in the car (lounges on the shelf near the back window); her blue and pink toy mouse.

Dislikes: Anyone else but Audrey; not getting enough attention; not being taken along in the car.

Hobbies: Hiding important household items (eg keys) underneath the floorboards or settee.

Audrey and Jasmine.

happens is that I put out some food for her, go up to bed and crash out. Then she comes up the stairs a few minutes later and breathes cat food all over me.'

It was nearing the end of June, 1996, and Audrey had been putting in a typical nursing week. 'I was generally working a 12-hour shift, 70-hour week,' she explains. 'I'd get home about nine o'clock, totally zonked.' On this particular evening, the day had been particularly tiring, and when Audrey stepped in through the front door, she could think of nothing else but clambering into bed. 'The thing about me is that I hate to go to bed unless I absolutely have to,' explains Audrey. 'I like to wait until I'm completely exhausted before I go to sleep.'

Audrey hung up her coat, kicked the draught excluder across the bottom of the door, and made her way to the kitchen. After putting out Jasmine's food, the prospect of making a cup of tea seemed too Herculean by half, instead Audrey climbed the small wooden staircase up to her bedroom, and went to bed straightaway. Soon Jasmine was there with her. 'She was so pleased to see me that evening,' remembers Audrey. 'Dead affectionate, as ever.' It wasn't long

Audrey will always remember what Jasmine did.

before Audrey was out like a light, fast asleep.

For most people, the sound of an alarm clock is more than enough to provoke a response. Some people wake up, and slap on the snooze button, as long as there is one. Others simply pick up the offending object and throw it firmly at a wall. In today's stressful lifestyle, there are also those who find it difficult to fall asleep at all, people who, even if they do find slumber, are easily woken by the slightest noise.

Not so Audrey. She is notorious among her friends, colleagues and family as being one of the deepest sleepers in Britain. 'When Audrey goes to sleep,' explains her mother, 'she sleeps the sleep of the dead. I've actually shaken her, physically shaken her, and not been able to wake her up.' When Audrey was studying to become a nurse, she became well-known for her uncanny ability to sleep through fire alarms. 'The bell was right next to my room,' she remembers, 'but there were four or five alarms that I just slept right through. It was only when firemen saw me dozing that they believed me.' When Audrey is on a day shift, it is customary for the sisters to give her a wake-up call, as the three alarm clocks she possesses are rarely enough to rouse her.

This made it all the more puzzling to Audrey when she opened her eyes in the middle of the night. It was dark in her bedroom. Her mind was befuddled with sleep. Perhaps she was still dreaming. But she could hear a noise, pervading her consciousness. As she listened, it became unmistakeable. It was a scream.

'It was Jasmine,' remembers Audrey. 'She hardly even purrs normally but she was downstairs making this screaming, shrieking noise.' Still hazy, Audrey rose unsteadily to her feet and staggered to the light. But when she flicked the switch, the bulb stayed dark. Confused and still half-asleep, Audrey staggered back to her bed, and flopped down onto the covers once more. Whatever it was, it could wait until morning.

But the screaming did not stop. 'Most of the time, I just won't get up for anything,' explains Audrey. 'But I started thinking, maybe Jasmine's in some kind of pain. So I clambered over to the light again.'

She flicked the switch for a second time. Still no response from the bulb. But as she glanced up at the fixture, she could see something. A distant, orange glow. The light, in the darkness. With horrifying clarity, Audrey suddenly realised that there was nothing wrong

Damage from the fire was severe, the television completely melted away (above).

with the bulb at all. The reason she could not see it was because the room was full of smoke.

A thick, black, poisonous cloud had filled the room. Even Audrey's bare 100 watt light bulb had trouble penetrating it. Audrey moved to the heavy curtains, and pulled them aside.

The inside of her window was caked with soot. She wiped her hand across it, and daylight poured into the room. Dawn was already breaking outside - it was only the smoke that was making the room so dark. There was no doubting it now. Her house was on fire.

Audrey screamed for Jasmine, and rushed to the top of the stairs. There, she was met by a searing heat from below, making it impossible to go on. 'I couldn't see my hand in front of my face,' recalls Audrey. 'The stairs were acting like a chimney, they were just completely caked in soot. I could hear Jasmine trying to scramble up the stairs to me, and then tumbling back down. The heat was just too much for her.'

Jasmine had been trapped downstairs on one of her nightly visits to her litter tray in the kitchen. Now, try as she might, it seemed there was no way of getting back to Audrey.

'I ran back to the window,' remembers Audrey, 'but it wouldn't open. So I just put my fist right through the centre of the pane.' Audrey cleared the glass away with her foot and gulped in the fresh air. 'I called out for Rob, who lives next door,' continues Audrey. 'Then I ran back to the landing to try again.'

The top of the stairs was now completely consumed with smoke.

'The first I heard of it were these noises from next door,' remembers Rob. 'I was still half asleep so I didn't know what it was. Then when I heard Audrey scream I realised I wasn't dreaming. It was then that I called the fire brigade.'

The top of the stairs was now completely consumed with smoke. Jasmine's panicked mews were still ringing in her ears, but there was no way Audrey could reach her cat. Downstairs, she could hear breaking glass and crackling sounds. She ran back to the window once more. 'I could see Rob, Dave, and Anita, two other neighbours from either side,' Audrey recalls. 'And Rob was just screaming, "jump lass, jump!", and I was shouting "but Jasmine woke me up!". In the end I just jumped.'

Leaping from the first floor, she was caught by Dave. Meanwhile Jasmine's cries could still be heard from inside. Thinking quickly, Audrey shouted over to

Rob to fetch his spare keys. 'It's a very neighbourly street,' she explains. 'Everyone looks after everyone else.' Rob returned with the set and together with Audrey made his way towards the front door. By now, Jasmine's mews were growing weaker and weaker, and the two rescuers knew that time was running out. But when they opened the door, the flames erupted with the added oxygen, and Rob slammed the door shut quickly. There was no way they could get to Jasmine now.

Within seconds, the paramedics had arrived, closely followed by members of the Green Watch of nearby Birkenhead fire brigade. 'They took me to the ambulance, and put an oxygen mask on me,' remembers Audrey, 'but I was just screaming: "Go and get Jasmine!"'

As Audrey was rushed away to hospital, the remaining witnesses stood by helpless as the firemen connected their pipes to the water supply. By now Jasmine's cries had stopped. Everyone's hearts were in their boots.

And it was then that a member of the Green Watch team stepped in. Wearing his respiration equipment, he quickly gained access to the house. It was only a matter of seconds before he emerged with a grey bundle of fur in his arms: jet black with soot, limp, but alive. Audrey's rescuer had been rescued.

'Jasmine saved my daughter's life, I have no doubt about that,' explains Audrey's mum Marion. 'She's the only thing that would have woken her. They are very close so I suppose it's a bit like being attuned to your own child's cry.'

Audrey is just as grateful: 'I know for a fact that I would not have woken up if it hadn't been for Jasmine,' she agrees. 'She's a cat in a million.'

Useful addresses

Royal Society for the Prevention of Cruelty to Animals
Causeway
Horsham
West Sussex
RH12 1HG

People's Dispensary for Sick Animals
Whitechapel Way
Prior's Lee
Telford
Shropshire
TF2 9PQ

PRO Dogs
6 New Road
Ditton
Kent
ME20 6AD

Blue Cross Animal Welfare
Shilton Road
Burford
Oxon
OX18 4PF

Support Dogs
PO Box 447
Sheffield
F6 6YZ

Battersea Dogs Home
4 Battersea Park Road
London
SW8 4AA

National Animal Welfare Trust
Tyners Way
Watford Bypass
Watford
WD2 8HQ

National Canine Defence League
17 Wakeley St.
London
EC1V 7LT

Cats Protection League
17 Kings Road
Horsham
West Sussex
RH13 5PN

CHATA
Children in Hospital and Animal Therapy Association
87, Longland Drive,
Totteridge,
London N20 8HN

Guide Dogs For The Blind
Hillfields
Burghfield Common
Reading
Berks
RG7 3YG

These are just a few of the many organisations committed to the health and welfare of pets in this country and abroad.

Acknowledgements

A big thank you to Emma Callery, Jerry Goldie, Penny Simpson, Fiona MacIntyre and everyone else at Ebury; a bouquet to Meridian Broadcasting; medals of honour to Sallie Clement, Sally Lindsay and the rest of the 'Pet Power' production team; certificates of special merit to David Jackson and the Prospect Multimedia team; and first class rosettes to helpful friends, family and pets. Thank you also to Tania Mitchell of the Blue Cross charity; Justine Pannett of the RSPCA; Christopher Lohan and Pippa Strutt of Aspect Communications; Spillers Pet Foods; Val Strong; Sandra Stone; Rona Brown, animal consultant; and Kevin MacNicholas and Robert Killick.

Picture credits

p.9 by Clive Dixon © Rex Features; pp.20, 21 by Ron Lane; pp.45, 47 © West of England Newspapers; pp. 67, 70 by John Griffin © Ebury Press; p.79 by John Sherbourne © Daily Mail; p.115 © Eastern Daily Press; p. 122 © Liverpool Daily Post and Echo. Video stills © Meridian Broadcasting 1997. All other pictures were supplied by the pet owners or by Prospect Pictures.

THE AUTHORS

Tess Cuming and David Wolstencroft are co-creators of Pet Power, a Prospect Pictures production for Meridian Broadcasting and the ITV Network.